THE SECRET PLACE

Intimacy with God

Woody Money

ISBN: 1530496020
ISBN 13: 9781530496020
Library of Congress Control Number: 2016904446
CreateSpace Independent Publishing Platform
North Charleston, South Carolina

Preface

This book comes from a desperate search for genuine lasting freedom. Honestly, I haven't always searched for it. I guess I really didn't believe it existed. As a kid, I struggled with anxiety, depression, and addiction that followed me into adulthood—but no one knew. I wondered many times if the chains that held me were a normal part of living. Sin, addiction, and emotional bondage are just a normal part of life...right? I walked through thoughts of suicide and anxiety, feeling so overwhelmed and alone. The questions became: *Who do I turn to? Who can I trust? Will they judge me?* With seemingly nowhere else to turn, I turned deeper into secret sin for a try at freedom—sin that led to shame, which only led to more sin, more anxiety, and more shame.

As a pastor, spiritual warfare can be a constant intense battle. Inside I've felt a roller coaster of emotions as I wade through everybody's problems, struggle to maintain a relationship and influence with my team, and attempt to balance it all with family time. Insecure thoughts like, *I wonder why they don't like me?* and, *I wonder if that speech went well?* have hijacked most evenings when I try to relax. The temptation has been to always turn to a bottle or to some other source of temporary relief...anything to make the anxiety go away. As in my childhood, I began to believe anxiety and bondage were just a normal part of living.

The book you are holding is a culmination of my search through many boxes of paper that I've never been able to throw away. Finding myself trapped and desperate for answers, I began sifting through these boxes to discover how I became free many years ago in hopes that maybe I could stay free the rest of my life. While going through these boxes, I discovered an intense desire to record and communicate this journey to freedom to my kids. I thought perhaps they too could find freedom and stay free, if only I could find the secret and put it on paper. Ironically, I found in Psalm 91 (my granddad's favorite chapter in the Bible) that God would speak of a *secret* place…the *secret* I was looking for.

The *secret* place I discovered has changed everything for me. It feels as if God is breathing fresh life into me every day. I want to shout, laugh, and cry for joy all at the same time! I have truly found a place of real *lasting* freedom, far above all depression, shame, and bondage to sin. I believe few truly find this place. Imagine living your entire life in a boring warehouse, believing that there is nothing more than four concrete walls. What would it feel like to discover the door and go outside for the first time? In the secret place there is an undiscovered world of freedom to awaken to in your heart.

This book is a confession, a guide, and a journey to that secret place. It is full of personal stories, experiences, biblical truths, and practical how-to sections. Through these pages, I want to communicate the love between Christ and His Church and lead you to the secret place in a practical way.

The secret place of my freedom is in His arms of intimacy. I truly believe this book is a doorway to your own intimacy with Him and to genuine lasting freedom and fulfillment. Let's begin our journey.

Dedication

I "lub" you, Jessica. I dedicate this book to you. You overwhelmingly deserve it. Your love, patience, and support through uncharted waters have given me a freedom in Christ greater than I could have ever hoped for without you. You've picked me up every time I was discouraged. You've held my hand when it felt as though I were alone. You've stood by me on the unpaved, dangerous road of unpopular opinion. You've challenged me at my worst and cheered at my best. You've shown me the love of a bride—*the* Bride—and that family is what really matters in life. Without you, I would be a "lost Christian," serving religion, works, and legalism. I love you, J-Money, Ziva. Thank you for loving me "for better or for worse."
—Woody

Contents

Introduction:

The Dream

Throughout the Bible, dreams are often God's choice for communication with people. Consider Daniel, Joseph, Solomon, Pharaoh, and Pilate's wife, just to name a few. In the following instance, He possibly did this with me, not because I'm special, but because sleep was about the only time He could get me to listen...a time when I had no choice but to listen. This dream would change my life and, as you read, I hope yours as well.

The dream began outside of an old white wooden house. The house was weathered, with chipped paint on the door and sides of the house, well-worn from use. I entered the house through the front door, and directly ten feet in front of me was another door, which was open. Inside this open door was a dimly lit room—a bedroom. Jesus walked into the house behind me. He walked right through me and into this bedroom. I felt in my heart that I should follow Him, but instead I turned and crept down a narrow hallway to my right. At the end of this hall was a kitchen, where I prepared a small tub of water to begin cleaning the house.

Immediately when I woke up, the Lord spoke to me, saying, "The Church is in the kitchen, while I am in the bedroom." He then said, "They have traded intimacy with Me for their own works." As I lay there, the Lord began revealing to me in my heart how some Christians have loved working for Him (the kitchen) more than they have loved intimacy *with* Him (the bedroom).

To work for God is very rational to the human mind. It's not hard for a believer to wrap his or her mind around rescuing the poor, healing the sick, or radically memorizing scripture. What is most difficult to rationalize is a deeply intimate relationship with God. Oftentimes, it appears easier to love God's work, which we can see, more than God Himself, who is typically "unseen."

Many of us have thought at one time or another that to interact with God is optional. The unfortunate belief is that interaction with Him seems to happen for some people, and for others, it doesn't—as if there were some sort of super-elite version of Christianity that some of us are fortunate to get, while others are stuck with a "normal" life. The wonderful truth is that God wants us to experience and interact with Him no matter where we come from and no matter who we are. He wants us to know Him. By intentional design, He is to be the closest person to our hearts and wants to have an intimate relationship with us, one on one. He doesn't want us to be workers for Him. He wants us to be His Bride—not in a weird sexual way, but in an intimate, loving, and united way. He doesn't need a maid; He needs a wife.

Intimacy with God begins with understanding His heart for you. Have you ever been forced to spend time with someone you loathe? Maybe on the playground as a kid? You know that one kid who always had a booger to put on you? I have great news! To God, you aren't the booger kid who He can't get away from. He doesn't just love you enough to die for you; He actually adores you…and He likes you. He loved you even before He sent His son to die for you (see John 3:16). It doesn't matter how much you've messed up in life; He doesn't hold it against you. In fact, He doesn't remember it: "I, even I, am He who blots out your transgressions, for My own sake, and remembers your sins no more" (Isa. 43:25). He sees you as a brand new person (2 Cor. 5:17). He is a Husband who loves His beautiful, spotless Bride—you—unconditionally (Eph. 5:25–27; Isa. 54:5; Rom. 8:38–39). He is calling you to a secret place with Himself.

He wants to be embraced by every believer in intimacy. However, most people never get to know what it is to truly live in the arms of Jesus—to be a passionate "lover" of Christ. Again, please remember that I am *not* referring to sex with God—that would be weirder than Russel Crowe riding a unicycle on the sun. God is calling you to a level of great intimacy with Him that is emotional, conversational, and for the most part incredibly far above human thought and understanding. In scripture, this place of intimacy is known as "the secret place"—a place talked about in Psalm 91.

I am in no way saying that I have become or will ever become an expert on this subject. What I am hoping, however, is that the many years of writing about what I have learned and experienced in the secret place will help you on your journey. The first half of this book explains my own journey from being a worker for God to coming ever closer to becoming the intimate Bride of Christ we are all called to be. In the second half of this book, as we dive into the secret place, I will share strategies on how to activate your intimacy with God in very practical ways.

To assist you in this journey to the secret place, I have included helpful tasks for you, such as reading and prayer. Thank you so much for joining me on this journey and reading this book. Welcome to my passion. Welcome to the secret place. Take it slow and enjoy.

1

Out of the Kitchen

If I were a fish, I would consider street ministry to be water. It's a major part of what I feel I was spiritually born to do and to thrive in. I will never forget the first time I ever prayed for a stranger in the streets. I was sitting in my car in my driveway listening to a CD: *Prophetic Evangelism* by Sean Smith. I had recently attended one of his conferences and purchased over $350 worth of CDs, DVDs, and reading material. I was so moved that I bought one of everything he had on his table! I was getting married in a few months, and we really could not afford this purchase. Calling my soon-to-be wife, Jess, to tell her how much I spent was a fun-filled learning experience.

That day I was listening for what must have been the tenth time to that series on evangelism—begging God to break my heart for the lost. I remember Sean Smith saying, "Weepers will be reapers." I began to cry uncontrollably. I begged God to use me. Just by being open and honest with Him, in the middle of my sobbing I heard in my heart, "Orange shirt, Wal-Mart." It sounded like a thought, but the thought seemed different in some way. I sat stunned for a second, looking out the window of my car. I noticed an orange arrow on the road that a surveying company had put there. Anxiously, I backed my car out of my driveway and headed toward Wal-Mart.

I was nervous, but at the same time, I was so incredibly desperate to be used by God that I was OK with looking like a crazy person—fear of that didn't bother me at this point. I wanted God to use me more than I wanted to appear sane. As I reached Wal-Mart, I *heard* God say as a thought again, "Everything with his dad is going to be all right." As I topped the hill at Wal-Mart, the first person I saw in the parking lot was a little girl in an orange shirt following her mom. I then noticed a man in a bright orange vest getting shopping carts out of the parking lot. I wondered if this man could be the person God was talking about who was at Wal-Mart with an orange shirt and had problems with his dad. I parked near him and got out of my car.

As I walked toward him, I wasn't sure what to say, so I said the only thing I could think of: "I was sent here to tell you something." He must've thought I was a hit man about to kill him with my hands in the pockets of my huge black leather jacket. I then said, "Everything with your family is going to be all right." He just looked shocked at me—his eyes wide and his mouth dropping open. I continued: "Specifically with your dad." So there we stood, silent, just staring at each other—both a little freaked out.

After a few seconds, he said, "Who sent you here, and how do you know about that?" I told him how I was sitting in my car praying and God told me to drive across town just to tell him that. He replied, "Well, I just found out today that my dad of eighteen years is not my real dad." I replied, "Wow. Well, God loves you so much, He told me to drive across town just to tell you that. That was God on the outside—do you want to know God on the inside?" He said yes, and right there he gave his life to Jesus in the parking lot. My whole life was forever changed.

NEED A HAT?
Shortly after this experience, Jess and I were married. I took every ministry position I was offered and went anywhere I might have few minutes to serve. I was also offered tons of speaking engagements. You might say I was a "man of many hats." I was heavily involved with a ministry on campus called "XA." I was also a full-time student, a coworship leader, an international student ministry coleader, and the outreach coordinator.

I led worship at a youth group that was a forty-five minute drive away and also led the Bible study for them on some nights. On top of all this, I went to two other Bible studies during the week, and I was also in charge of the message sign and children's ministry at my church. I was out every night, either on the streets or in the church. From the time the sun came up to around midnight or one o'clock in the morning, I preached on the streets, wrote sermons, taught lessons from the word, led worship, or led outreach. Oh, and did I mention that I had three part-time jobs?

At this point in my life, I didn't understand the concept of "balance"—which thankfully I would later learn. I hadn't learned yet that life is full of priorities and that those priorities have an order. Being married, I had a priority at home that I'd begun to let slip—my relationship with my wife, my parents, and my sister.

Nearly every night, my best friend William and I hit the streets in prophetic street evangelism. We saw deaf ears made whole, arms that had been completely crushed restored, blind eyes open, a torn rotator cuff completely mended in Wal-Mart, and tumors healed. Among the miracles, we saw arms, legs, backs, hips, mental illness, and bondages to sin healed immediately. Many people gave their heart to Jesus on the spot. I have page after page full of the miracles we saw in the streets during that time. I can remember asking to pray for an old man I saw with a cane, and he said to me, "Oh, you're one of those active Christians." That comment really ticked me off! I thought to myself, *What the heck is a nonactive Christian?* Needless to say, I was what he called "active."

God did some very amazing things during this time, although my life was incredibly out of balance. Looking back now, I can see that being in the street with William was what God had called me to do at this time—although not until after midnight. I can also see that God wanted me to be a coworship leader at the campus ministry I was involved in. However, when I consider the half dozen other ministry opportunities I was presented with, I now can see that I should have said *no*. Soon you will realize why.

THE BATTLEFIELD

My wife and I gradually lost touch as the late nights out became more frequent. Over time, we drifted far from the intimate fire we had shared when we were first married. We argued more, with each quarrel growing in intensity. I believe, for a time, that it may have seemed to her as if "Jesus" was stealing her husband. My mind constantly raced with ideas of what to do next for God, while her mind constantly raced with ideas of what to do with me—where we could go or have fun together. Deep down I wanted to be a good husband, but I didn't see how it fit in my life's bubble. I couldn't see how it fit in my life's "calling." At the time I thought, *Every moment I spend at home is a moment I could've been somewhere else doing something for God.* I was trapped in sort of an unbalanced "battlefield." I was constantly in a fight.

I remember on my way to a Bible study late one night feeling a tug in my heart that I should go home to my wife. I remember this same feeling happening on many nights when it would get late. I would often feel convicted about being out at all hours. However, I always convinced myself that those feelings were just the demonic realm trying to get me to somehow miss an opportunity for God to "show up."

Gradually, I began believing thoughts like, *I would be better off without her, She just slows me down,* and *I need a woman who loves God*—never realizing that I already had a woman who loved God waiting for me at home. I remember even one moment thinking, *Am I called to lose my wife for Jesus?* Now, obviously this thought was not from God, but I had numbed myself to that area of my heart. No matter how hard God was trying to fix my marriage, I always assumed it was the devil interfering. Sure, I could hear the voice of God to see ministry happen, and I knew that God was constantly doing something everywhere we looked. But what I didn't know was how to tell the difference between what He wanted me to do and what He wanted someone else to do. Therefore, I did what He called me to do and then attempted to do everything else!

During this busy time, my wife would often say things like, "I wish you were home more," and "We need 'us' time." In my mind, these comments were what I considered to be a form of weak Christianity. I would retort with "religious" things like, "There are people out there waiting for the Lord to show up," and "If you can't get on board, then get off!" During this time, though we lived in the same apartment building, I became a stranger to my sister and my parents, who rarely saw me. I had to walk by my family's apartment door to get to mine. Despite that fact, I rarely visited, stopping by primarily when I needed money or a favor.

THE PRICE TO PAY?

I once encouraged a young man for hours after a ministry service where I led worship on campus. To reiterate, God wanted me to lead worship that night; however, He did not want me to do what I'm about to describe. For hours and hours we talked, and all the while it got later and later and later. He told me about him witnessing to people on the Internet in chat rooms. He mentioned the doubts and fears he had about his faith. He praised me for how cool I was for talking with him and what a good friend I was. Keep in mind, it was getting late—my meeting was over hours ago. As I'm writing this, I can just picture God in that particular moment screaming, "GO HOME TO YOUR WIFE!" I will never forget what happened next...

As we sat on the tailgate of that young man's truck at two in the morning in front of his dorm on campus, I actually saw my wife's car drive by. She was out frantically looking for me. I never called her to tell her I was going to be late or to even tell her where I was. All this time, her fears had been growing and growing as to where in the world I was. I was so worried about this young man's fears while totally shutting out the Holy Spirit urgently knocking about my wife's fears about whether I was OK or who I might be with! But none of that mattered to me. I thought to myself, *It's just the price she has to pay to follow Jesus.* It was as if I had shut down the "go home" call of the Holy Spirit. I should've gone home after our campus ministry was over, but I saw a need and thought, *Hey there's a need. God must want me to fill it!* I couldn't have been more wrong. At this point in my life, I could see that much work needed to be done for the kingdom of God. However, I had no idea of His heart for how to accomplish it. I had no bearing on how to be a husband to my wife and the Bride of Christ at the same time.

Later that night, I went home feeling great about what God was doing in that young man's life. The only explanation I gave for myself when I got home was that I had to "minister" to someone. I gave no apology to my wife whatsoever. Hell hath no fury like a woman scorned...*crazy fiery hellish fury*. She had a right to be upset. Of course, many "religious" folk might argue that I had done nothing wrong. It could be argued that there is a cost involved with ministering the gospel. However, your ministry should never come before your spouse and family. They are, in fact, your first ministry. God will never ask you to sacrifice them.

My lack of intimacy with God left me in a "kitchen" of works. I spent every waking moment in the "kitchen" working for God. I knew that there was a ton of work to do for God. Unfortunately, I didn't give Him much of a chance to speak to me on how to balance it with what I was first called to do with my family.

I can remember coming home from one of those late-night Bible studies and seeing Jess lying in our bed with the lights off. For a moment, I thought, *It would be a good thing to get in bed with her; I know she doesn't like falling asleep alone.* I immediately stopped that thought, considering all the work that was left to be done for God. I turned around and walked into the living room, where I stayed up late writing about what God had done that day, hoping that someday someone would read it. I eventually fell asleep on the couch and never came to bed at all. There were tons of nights just like that. It was a cycle: come home late from some sort of ministry...write for hours...pass out on the couch...wake up around 2:00 a.m. and go to bed...and repeat the next day.

I can remember waking up at three in the morning to pray. A few times after I got up, I ran cold water over my head in the bathtub just so I could stay awake to pray for revival. While waking up early and praying was God's heart for me, it wasn't His heart that I spend all night in the living room while my wife yet again fell asleep alone in bed. I couldn't tell the difference between what God would be pleased with me doing and what I shouldn't do. I didn't give Him a chance to speak concerning the subject. I think in some way it scared me to think of Him saying, "Stop." Deep down, I believe I feared that somehow I wouldn't reach my destiny if I "slowed down." I thought that somehow I wouldn't become "important." I feared that my desire to become a "revivalist" would be in jeopardy if I didn't do "everything I could" with every waking moment. I had decided that there was a price to pay to serve God! In my mind, people who "wasted time" at home were lazy. Sadly, I inwardly judged some of my friends who weren't as zealous and "active" as I was. I had decided that I was a soldier of God and that I was to fight constantly! Ironically, it was my lack of intimacy with the God I was fighting for that was ultimately leading me to divorce.

NEVER ALONE
I came home around midnight one night and found Jess crying, with her head between her knees, in our dimly lit hallway. "Never Alone" by Barlow Girl was blaring out of the radio in the bathroom. What could I do? What could I say? I could say, "I'm sorry!" At the time I didn't believe I was in the wrong. I don't remember saying anything to her that night, but I can remember many nights like this one where we fought so hard.

As I pulled out of the driveway to go do "work" for God extremely late one night, I heard God say in my heart, "If you leave, you will never see her again." In that moment, I saw Jess out of the corner of my eye coming to the window of my car. I let the window down to hear her say, "If you leave, I won't be here when you get back." I let up the window and pulled out of the driveway. I have no idea what I must have been thinking in that moment. Perhaps I was full of pride. Perhaps, yet again, I entertained the thought that I was supposed to lose her if I was to follow Christ. I didn't want to lose her! However, the painful question still remained. I left and went to yet another Bible study or on another inner-city crusade. When I came back, her car was gone. I freaked out and spent a long time trying to find her. I began to pray in the house, begging God to bring her home. Thank God for His grace. When she eventually did come home, she told me that God had spoken to her and comforted her—changing her mind about leaving. As we stood just inside the doorway in the dark, we hugged and cried together.

I didn't notice it at the time, but the results of my out-of-balance actions were the same as if I were a drunk, a cheat, or a crackhead—intense fights with my wife about staying out all night and neglecting her and my family. The results of my actions were as though I were "lost." Many of the noble deeds and late nights I so highly exalted were ruining my life. But why?

One late night, I asked God through tears, "Why is everything going wrong when I am doing all of this stuff for You?" I was on my way to one of my three Bible studies that week.

His response surprised me. He said, "I never asked you to do some of those things." For the first time in my life, I began to realize that God has a specific destiny for my life. I started to see that anything outside that destiny puts my life out of balance. I realized that a lot of the ministry I did during that time was in God's plan for my life, while at the same time, much of it wasn't.

With this new revelation beginning to work in my life, I very slowly began the bittersweet process of gaining a healthy pace. What I would learn is that I could do more for the Lord by only doing what was asked of me by the Spirit of God than by trying to save the world by myself.

THE DOOR
It wasn't long before God gave me the dream I spoke of in the introduction. Remember the Lord's words spoken in that dream, "The Church is in the kitchen, while I am in the bedroom. They have traded intimacy with Me for their own works." As I stood there in the kitchen in my dream, preparing a tub of water to begin cleaning the house, I noticed something very crucial. As I looked up from the washbasin, I noticed a door right in front of me. This door led directly from the kitchen to the bedroom, the secret place. As I began to develop real Intimacy with God, He began to change my life forever. By letting God change your life through this book,

you are following me through that door. Whether you're a brand-new believer or you've been in the "kitchen" your whole life, it is the perfect time to become intimate with your creator. I encourage you to be brave as you read the rest of this book. Let's go!

NEXT: A PATH TO FREEDOM

During one of my visits with my parents at their home in Jacksonville, Florida, I helped my dad build a concrete path. My dad once told me that every time he went to his dad's house, he was doing projects around the house. I laughed and thought to myself, *Funny how that stuff is generational.* I don't consider it a curse, though. It is a blessing to give back to my parents. I could never repay all that they have done to help us. It's an honor to serve them.

The journey in pulling this path out of me has taken a lot of digging. Just like that concrete path my dad and I built, it has been dirty and difficult at times. However, I've loved every minute of it and had the best for company. The next portion of this book describes a path—a path of my journey to the secret place with God. I hope to help you see how the calling to intimacy with Him has been battled for over time.

I have split up this path to intimacy into chapters 2 and 3. With this path I hope to show you the struggle every Christian faces...caught between influences of the kingdom of light and the demonic realm.

I hope you find comfort in that you, too, can find intimacy with God, no matter who you are or what you've done. He is, in fact, warring for your intimacy from the time you are born to this very moment. This is my attempt to be as raw and real as possible. Please show me grace. I appreciate your letting me share my deepest struggles with you.

2

The Path, Part 1

Most people have a predominate sin that they've had to overcome in their lives (I do, and I'm sure you do as well)—a sin that speaks louder than others in an individual. For some, it's gambling; for others, it may be gluttony or drugs. My drug was lust, sex, and pornography. In the next chapters, I hope to communicate the battle for my intimacy. God is fighting for your heart from the moment you are born to this very moment, but the devil is, too.

Like all stories, this one starts from the beginning—my childhood.

"IN WITH THE BOTTLE"

Mom took me to church one Saturday night when I was five years old to prepare for her Sunday school class that following morning. We went into the dark church, turned the lights on, and headed to her classroom. While she prepared her room, I sat quietly and waited. All of a sudden, my mom saw me run off. I was headed toward the back of the church. Calling after me, she asked me why I was going over there. I said, "A man called my name." She freaked out a little because there wasn't supposed to be anyone in there but us! We looked all over and couldn't find anyone.

When we talked to our pastor about it, he reminded us of the story of Samuel in the temple (1 Sam. 3:8–9) who also heard a voice call to him at a young age. He encouraged me from then on to reply to the voice: "Speak, Lord, for your servant is listening." From that day on, and for a long, long time, every time I lay down at night I would say that. From that moment on, I began to listen for God's voice. I realized He wanted to speak with me.

Concerned about this journey, my path, I recently told my mom that I was trying to find out where it started. I asked, "Why do I love Jesus like I do today?"

Her response was, "Honey, it goes in with the bottle."

Looking back now, I see that this is so true. After asking her what she meant, she told me that from the moment I was born, I was given videos and music that all pointed to Jesus. She said every minute I was watching something else was a minute I could be watching something about Jesus. My dad and mom were very intentional about their kid's relationship with Jesus. As the bottle was given us, so was the love of Jesus. "Train up a child in the way he should go: and when he is old, he will not depart from it" (Prov. 22:6 KJV).

My parents positioned me to burn spiritually. Just as Isaac was placed on the altar by Abraham, his father, so too did my parents place me on the altar of God's presence to burn for Him. Good parenting is all about pouring out your child's life as a sacrifice to God. My childhood was surrounded by God. Almost every craft, every video game, every type of media was about God. My mom got me a Carman cassette when I was little. I remember jumping around and rapping (I so wish I had a video of this). Either way, I was on the altar. It's funny to listen to Carman now that music has changed so drastically.

Every night before bed, I tell my kids a list of biblical truths, and I get them to repeat them back to me. Jess and I always remind them of who they are (their identity in Christ) and try to prepare them to walk into their future. Even as young as our kids are, we tell them what kind of spouse they should marry. The reality is this: what you prepare your kids for is what they will be able to walk in to. Consider David and his son Solomon. David told his son to do whatever he could do to get wisdom and to hold on to it. When Solomon was later offered by God to receive anything he asked for, he asked for wisdom. Because Solomon chose wisdom, he became the wisest, richest, and most powerful man on the earth. Because of his father's preparation, Solomon grasped his future. Again, what you prepare your kids for is what they will walk into. (See 1 Kings 3 and Prov. 4)

Among the many things we speak about to our kids, one is that they should talk to Jesus. Recently, my oldest daughter Madelyn (four years old at the time), while sitting in the bathtub with her younger sister Ava (one year old at the time), had a similar experience to mine when I was five. Madelyn sat up quick and attentive, as if puzzled and listening for something. She said, "Who's that talking real low?"

My wife answered, "What do you hear, baby?"

She replied, "Eve," and kept playing with Ava.

I asked her about it later, and she said she'd heard a man's voice. She said it was Jesus explaining how He made people, plants, and animals to Ava because, "She was little and didn't know anything." It's exciting to know that because of our preparation, God is speaking in an audible voice to our young children. Madelyn and Ava are listening for God's voice because they know He wants to interact with them. I challenge you to prepare your kids to achieve the impossible and see what happens.

ENCOUNTERING DEMONS WEARING DIAPERS

When I was around six years old, Mom hung a picture of Jesus in my bedroom. I would stare at that picture for sometimes fifteen to thirty minutes at a time while I lay in my bed. Often I would stare at it so long, it looked like it was moving. I made sure that picture was the last thing I was looking at when I closed my eyes to go to sleep. Whenever I accidentally opened my eyes, I would lean forward and close my eyes again while looking at the picture. Unfortunately, that's not all that went on in my bedroom at night. Parents so often drastically underestimate demon's interactions with their children. At night at six years old, I was tortured on my bed. I had the most horrible dreams. I dreamed that I was in hell. At this age, I don't think I even knew exactly what hell was…but I was there, and my parents were dead. I can still smell that place and feel the intense heat. I was told to find my parents in cardboard boxes. I looked frantically but could not find them. They were gone forever. When I woke, I ran to my parents and cried and hugged them. This is the first dream I can remember having.

The second dream I remember was very similar. I encountered a demon I tried to scare away. When I yelled at her, I heard the word "LUST," and everything went black as white eyes flashed before my face. It felt as though many people were hitting me at once. For the first time I heard a sound that got so painfully loud, I had to kick myself awake to make it quit. This sound would haunt me for years.

On top of these dreams, I began to encounter demons almost every single night. I believe it was in connection with this experience that I first discovered sexuality. I wasn't molested or exposed to pornography. My parents didn't watch bad movies. I was deceived by demons down a dark path that would lead me to addiction and worse later in life.

JESUS WAS A CARPENTER

While the devil was fighting for my soul, so was Christ. As a child, I loved to build stuff with wood. I knew that Jesus was a carpenter, and it made me feel connected with Him to think about that. I remember working on something on the floor in my room and seeing right in front of me the bottom of a white robe of some sort. I looked up, startled, only to see the wall and a picture of Jesus my parents had placed there—a picture of Him carrying the cross in pain. I remember this happening again while I was outside a few days later, building something on the back porch. Through this, I awakened to the fact that Jesus really was with me. While I had seen glimpses of Him, I could also see other things around me…things I couldn't explain.

I saw my first pornographic image a few days later at six years old. It *wasn't* on a computer, television, or in a magazine. It appeared out of thin air on the kitchen floor. I will never forget it. My whole family was eating dinner. I looked over and saw on the floor two people doing something I don't want to describe here. I had never seen anything like that before. It vanished and I told no one. I had no idea how to process what I'd just seen…and so I internalized it. I didn't realize it then, but just as Christ was creating moments of intimacy with me, the demonic realm became more and more determined to steal them.

THE BIBLE, THE BULLY, AND THE TEMPTER

My family always had a night during the week when we went through a workbook about the Bible. I remember always having a Bible—many of them, in fact. Even most of my video games and movies were Bible based. Once, when my mom was sick, I got around five of my favorite video games for my NES (yes, the original). I would walk into the room and say, "Mom! Can I have another?" I suppose she had saved them for Christmas and birthday presents. Giving them to me on that day, I suppose, gave me a way to relieve some energy and for her to get some rest.

My mom also gave us a ton of computer games that were Bible-based. I remember "Bible Man" and "Onesimus" in particular. "Bible Man" was incredible, because I actually got to help people with spiritual problems in the game. This was a huge growing point at that young age. It made me start thinking in a "loving people" sort of way. These games began to create a desire for God that I wasn't really aware of at the time; I just knew I was having fun. I remember reading my red children's Bible all the time, whether I understood it or not—the pictures inside made me want to read the stories. Even late at night, I can remember reading it.

While I did begin to learn to love people, a lot of times I was a bully to others, including my relatives. I got into so many fights on the playground at school. I've regretted being a bully over the years. I just hope that all those people know that I'm not like that anymore. As for my relatives, I love my awesome sister. We have a great relationship today. However, way back when we were kids, I was pretty horrible to her as well.

I sort of felt like I had to be a bully at school to survive. However, God was at work. Often I would pray for people at school to receive Christ in their hearts. In the third grade, I asked a kid on the bus, "Hey, you want to go to heaven?" When I said that, a kid behind me started repeating everything I said and laughed: "HA! HA! HA!" I turned around and said, "Shut up, this is serious!" I threatened to beat him up, turned back around, and led the kid beside me in the sinner's prayer.

That same year, my mom had "the talk" with me about sex. I guess I was asking a ton of questions, and most of my friends already knew, so she told me. I went to a couple of buddies the next day, so excited. I told them where babies come from...it was so fascinating to me. I got in so much trouble from their parents! Sex became the forbidden fruit, something that was a no-no, which only made me more curious. I began snooping in my parents' room for anything I could find related to sex. I found a science book that included human bodies, and I thought I had struck gold! I remember getting caught snooping pretty often and making up some excuse or another. My little picture Bible even became somewhat of a stumbling block to me, as some of those pictures were pretty provocative.

In the fifth grade I discovered the magazine rack at our local grocery store. I collected comic books, so it was easy for me to take a few glances at the men's magazines on display. I decided I would tear a few pages out of a Maxim magazine. The blood and sweat it took to get those pages without anyone in the whole store seeing or hearing...talk about a challenge. I felt like I was smuggling drugs. I took those pages to school to show my buddies. While I was showing them, a girl was looking over my shoulder and let out a shout. I freaked out so bad I ran out of the room screaming and tearing the pages to bits—yes, it was that bad. The janitor watched as the door to class burst open and I threw giblets of a half-naked woman in his trash can...he had to have found this hilarious. My friend William came to the bathroom and got me. He told everyone to leave me alone. This is one of my many face-palm moments.

PAUL

All this time the demonic realm was pulling hard on me as a young man, God was also pulling me to intimacy with Him. Between eight and ten years old, I recall weeping in my room many times, crying out to God. Screaming through tears and punching my bed, on my hands and knees, I begged God: "I want to be the next Paul!" I thought to myself, *I really don't know what all that means, but I want it.* I can remember feeling an awareness of the presence of God so strong in moments like that one—I could feel such an awe of God. In moments like this, my body would begin to shake. I believe that the Holy Spirit placed that great desire in my heart, even if I didn't understand it totally. Looking back, I wonder if my parents or my sister ever heard me praying. I'm sure they did.

In the seventh grade, I attended Crenshaw Christian Academy and took a class on the Bible. I loved this class. My parents had taught me a ton of stuff, so I was prepared to answer pretty tough questions. One day after class, my teacher pulled me aside. I had raised my hand in class and said that I saw someone glowing during chapel earlier that day. I remember seeing the person with light shining all around him. It was as if he had a spotlight shining from behind him. In that moment, she said something that would impact my life greatly. She said, "Woody, you're special—you are going to do great things for God someday." I don't remember what I said in return, but I remember feeling really good about it. That statement meant a lot to me and no doubt spoke to a desire in my heart God had placed there.

Around this time, I became so outraged about what my family was watching on TV. I remember one night pacing in my room getting madder and madder. My dad and sister were watching *COPS*, a law enforcement show. I heard the fighting and the partying that was happening on the show, and even though I'd never had a problem with it before, I couldn't bear it in that moment. Looking back now, I know the feeling I had was *conviction.* I ran into the living room, turned the TV off, and shouted, "If you don't want her doing that stuff when she gets older, then why are we watching a show about it?"

I recall such a sweet connection with God. I wrote songs and poetry to God at night in my room, often becoming overwhelmed by emotion and weeping. I never understood what was happening, but there were many moments like this that I spent aware of God's presence, moments that no doubt were pulling me to be intimate with Him.

GRANDDAD

When I was eleven years old, my paternal granddad (J. B. Money) passed away. I will always remember his favorite song. Some of the words were: "What a friend we have in Jesus, all our sins and grief to bear, what a privilege to carry everything to God in prayer." I had a book that my parents gave me and my sister that would play that song every time we pressed a button on the front. I'll never forget hearing that song at his funeral as my dad cried on my shoulder.

At this age and ever since, I have been inspired by my granddad's love for God. Everywhere I go, I hear stories about him. He has become almost legendary to me. I knew my granddad and knew he was a great man, and the stories I hear always amaze me. I recently heard a story of my granddad gathering Spanish moss off of trees, selling it, and then giving the money to his cousin so that he could afford books for school. My grandfather was a selfless man. He put others before himself—always. My dad told me he always "loved thy neighbor." Dad also told me he could hear him at night reading his Bible out loud—very loud—from his bed as my dad and his brother went to sleep. As it turns out, granddad's father (my great-granddad) read his Bible loudly on the edge of his bed at night as well.

I remember being told one story in particular about my granddad concerning the supernatural that would intrigue me deeply for many years to come. One evening, my granddad was driving in his truck in Saco, Alabama. An overfilled log truck in oncoming traffic lost control and began to jackknife into his lane. As the truck slid toward him, he saw the truck begin to turn over on top of him. When he yelled "Jesus!" the log truck—already at a steep angle to turn over—stopped sliding and rocked back down.

I will never forget the amount of honor my dad showed his dad when he shared his testimony at church one Sunday. I saw my dad, who has an incredible story of his own, begin to weep, saying, "I will never be the man he was." At that moment, though I heard what he said, I could *feel* something powerful in it. It was as if I felt it more than I could hear it. I could feel the presence and love of the Son. My dad believed in his dad and loved him very much.

When I think about my granddad, I think of the verse Hebrews 11:4 that says, "By faith Abel still speaks, even though he is dead." Surely because of his faith and love for God, the good things he did for others live on. My granddad is encouraging me through the mouths of others everywhere I go. His actions will speak to me and now to my kids and their children and their children's children—and to as many heirs as will hear this message. I also carry this mantle to my children, just as you can to yours—leaving a legacy of faith, hope, and love.

THE ALTAR

One Sunday, my entire family went to the altar for prayer. In that place, I could again feel something. God was healing us and loving on us, and I knew it. When we went back to our seats, I could see my parents weeping. This moment touched me more than they knew.

Throughout grade school, I always felt an urge to respond to the altar call. I went to pray at the altar whether or not I actually felt that I personally needed prayer for any particular thing. I would often go and just pray for my family. Many times I could hear God in my heart saying to go forward—that someone else in the congregation wanted to go for prayer but didn't want to go alone. And so I would go, just so others would feel more comfortable. I also remember going many times as a kid to the altar to pray for others who were already there.

THE TEMPTATION

Demons don't care about your age. They want to ruin you. The God moments I had as a child were surrounded by temptations of lust and sin. I began breaking into my neighbor's storage shed to steal lingerie magazines. My dad caught me with one—actually, my dad caught me with several, on many different occasions, and so did my mom. If you could somehow combine the words "awkward" and "terror," that's sort of a hybrid horrible definition of the way I felt about those experiences. The same feeling might accompany losing your bathing suit at the pool: sheer awkward terror.

Talking to girls became almost impossible after we got our first computer. I snuck around to watch all sorts of videos I shouldn't have. I would tilt the screen in my direction where they couldn't see it, mute the speakers, and watch whatever I wanted. My opinion and expectations of females began to change. My mind was always secretly going in inappropriate places. The worst videos would be late at night after my parents would go to sleep. I was secretly up half the night. It was around sixth and seventh grade that I, without actually saying it, made it my mission in life to have sex. Literally, that was my goal for living. Peer pressure was also so intense at this age. When every conversation in the locker room is about reproductive organs, what else was I supposed to look forward to? I would have thoughts like, *I don't think I will never get married and I will always be a loser.*

My feelings during this time are so difficult to describe. My feelings for God would be up one moment and down the next. I would be praying hard for my parents one second and cussing like a sailor the next. I prayed nightly for a relationship. I know now that deep down I wanted to be loved, and I wanted real intimacy. What I didn't know is that I would only scratch the surface of intimacy with random relationships that would come soon with college life. I needed the secret place, the intimate place of God.

FATHER HEART OF GOD
Around eleventh and twelfth grade I got more and more frustrated because I was girlfriendless. Despite my efforts, it seemed to me that I would be "forever alone." I didn't realize it, but this sent me into many moments of depression. Because of this depression, I began to rebel against the call of God on my life. I often would have arguments late at night with my parents about life. I cried and yelled around ten o'clock at night, at the foot of my parents' bed.

I told my dad, "Dad! Ain't nothing ever happened good to someone trying to be good!"

Dad replied, "Sonny boy, come here and sit by me." I did, and Dad said in a calm voice with his arm around me, "Don't ever say that, son."

In that moment, I was still discouraged about what seemed to me at the time to be my lack of success. I just sat there with him on the edge of the bed. I later would think about that moment often...it no doubt changed my life. He had seen me screw up and lash out at him so much, yet he loved and encouraged me. Looking back, I know I often could feel the Father Heart of God through my dad. Father God loved me, like my dad, despite my faults and reckless behavior. My dad was a constant lighthouse pointing to truth amid my storm.

My parents have shown me such a good example of who God is. I could hear Him clearly calling me because of who they are. Now, they would never admit that as true; they would probably tell you all of their faults. However, the truth is that we all view God in the beginning through the lens of our parents. Somehow, we all believe that God is like them—at least in the beginning. If your parents are generous, then you will have little trouble seeing that aspect of God. If your parents love the poor, then it probably won't be difficult to assume that about God. However, if your parents are distant, then you might assume God is also that way. If your parents are abusive, then you might also assume the same about God.

Today, I encourage you to contemplate what you believe God to be like. You might be assuming negative things about Him based on your experiences with your own parents. Please know that He is the perfect, fun, loving dad. It was this picture of God that I could see in my parents that helped me get through the next years of college, where I almost ended my life.

3

The Path, Part 2

Just as middle school is awkward for students, college can be just as awkward for young adults. In college, questions begin to surface in the heart: "Am I an adult now? Will I ever get married? Am I a loser?" These questions have such impact, that some students, myself included, will stop at nothing in attempting to answer them.

To answer these questions for myself, I began dating random girls, all while alienating myself from most of my friends. Eventually, I achieved my life goal: I became sexually active. I wondered, *I guess I'm a man now.* Surely the rite of passage to manhood had been achieved. Finally, I could command the same respect that my friends all walked in! Finally, I could hold my head high! I wondered if my friends would think I was a man now. Like everyone else, I bragged about it.

Unfortunately, being a "man" came with a price: I always worried if a random girl I had been with was pregnant. I would sweat bullets until I heard she was on her period. Sin causes paranoia, and I most certainly was paranoid out of my mind. This was no longer worry that my parents would find my porn stash or my secret Internet history. This was worry that my life would be ruined—or so I thought—by a child. In one of my lowest, most regrettable moments, I forced a girl to take a pregnancy test at a dirty, dimly lit gas station.

It wasn't long before one of those girls missed her period. Months earlier, I had sworn I would never ask for an abortion, but when my feet were put to the fire, that's exactly what I did...screaming it loud, violently arguing for it. At night, crying on my bedroom floor, alone and scared to death, I even begged God to kill the baby. I told Him I would never do it again...if He would just kill the baby. Who had I become? Where did the guy go who all the little old ladies of the church loved? Before long, I became partly responsible for both a miscarriage and an abortion. *Casual* porn had turned to *casual* sex, which had turned to *casual* death... I wanted to die. Suicidal thoughts became the norm as depression and condemnation constantly ran in to destroy me.

The sin of this period of my life followed me for years into my marriage even though I hadn't even known my wife during the time when the sin took place. Every TV commercial featuring kids, every mom with a stroller, every billboard and advertisement with babies, every single anti-abortion ad, made me feel pain so deep, I couldn't escape. I would often have dreams of children running in a field or myself pushing a coffin...and again, I wanted to die. Some nights I would lay down totally destroyed inside. I would cry myself to sleep, silently. My wife on the pillow beside me, facing the opposite direction, was possibly doing the same thing from the pain I was causing her (as described in the previous chapter). In fact, I know she did, as many nights I could hear the sniffles and tissues. Over time, somehow, she became an expert silent crier because of me. I often thought her crying was ridiculous...melodramatic...unwarranted. I was wrong. I often went to bed like that for years. It's crazy how your mind can run when you lay down. For people like me, it was a battle. The porn I secretly depended on and the sex I desired had come to collect payment. The Bible says that the wages of sin is death...how true this became.

In my early college life, I could always feel God's draw. Even at parties, I felt different. I understand now that the Father was literally "drawing" me to the secret place with Him. We know that no one comes to the Son unless the Father draws him. He was trying to rescue me. "For no one can come to Me unless the Father who sent Me draws them to Me, and at the last day I will raise them up. As it is written in the Scriptures, 'They will all be taught by God.' Everyone who listens to the Father and learns from Him comes to Me" (John 6:44–45 NLT). This was such an odd time. I began to do things I would never have thought to do before. I became so convicted by my sin, I couldn't even break the speed limit.

THE BEGINNINGS OF FIRE

My convictions almost led me to attack a man. A preacher came on campus, yelling at students, calling them all sorts of names. He called a group of girls whores. He called me and a few others a filthy brood of vipers. I got so mad, I almost attacked him. A girl ran up to me and told me he was a con artist and wasn't really a preacher. As I walked off, I remember breaking down. As I wept at a friend's house that night, I remember being called a "lunatic" for how broken I was about my sin. My friend told me to "get out!"

As I got in my car, I remembered that there was a college ministry small group meeting that night. I drove there, crying my eyes out. Suddenly, a song came to mind, and I began to sing: "Lord you are more precious than silver, Lord you are more costly than gold. Lord you are more beautiful than diamonds, and nothing I desire compares with you." As I sang that song, I felt God lift me and I became aware of His presence surrounding me. I had never been that aware of God's presence as I was in that moment. I didn't realize what was happening then, but I now know that King David went through moments where he would literally tell his soul to praise God whether he felt like it or not at the moment.

> Why, my soul, are you downcast? Why so disturbed within me? Put your hope in God, for I will yet praise Him, my Savior and my God. (Ps. 42:5)
>
> Bless the Lord, O my soul: and all that is within me, bless His holy name. Bless the Lord, O my soul, and forget not all His benefits. (Ps. 103:1–2 KJV)

Through those moments, David was lifted by the Lord. God was becoming everything to me as He drew me in more and more. I literally did not go looking for Him. He came and found me. That night in the car, God literally set my heart on fire. I felt for the first time in a long time that familiar fire I felt as a kid crying out to God on my bed. When I got to the small group, I could feel a tangible burning of His presence in my chest.

"I MAKE ALL THINGS NEW"

There comes a moment in everyone's life when we have to choose to surrender our wants, our desires, our everything to God's perfect will. Welcome to my "moment." It wasn't long before I went to a beach retreat in Panama City with that small group. We had a great time eating pizza mixed with sand on the beach. It was February, so getting in the water wasn't desirable—so naturally, I was thrown in by my friends. Chased down the beach by my campus pastor and his brother, they threw me in, yelling, "In the name of the Father, Son, and the Holy Spirit, I now baptize you!" It may be heresy, but I still consider that my baptism. As I looked around at my friends, I could see my family, people who cared about me and loved me, faults and all.

As I sat on that beach alone for hours after everyone left, I watched the sunset and turned my life over to Him. For the first time I really surrendered to his Lordship in my life. I read the creation story and the flood story again as if reading them for the first time. Not a cloud hung in the sky. Every glimmering star was visible. A perfectly crisp line from light to dark formed in the cold atmosphere. A single boat sat in the distance, silhouetted by a red-orange sunset. I wrote huge letters in the sand that said "I LOVE YOU" with a giant heart around them. In one moment, God said a thousand words that no preacher or teacher could utter. It felt like I could hear His voice and feel a loving, warm Father who was hugging me from the inside out. I was freezing on the beach but warm inside; every fiber of my being was alive. For the first time, every cell in my body was happy. For the first time in my life, I felt totally free from the bipolar relationship I'd had with God. I felt free just to love him.

I wept and worshiped, and I didn't care who watched. There I prayed that God would change the world with my life. As I looked back toward Panama City, I wept for people in sin. I was overwhelmed as I realized it was God's call on my life to awaken them. On the earth today, there is an army of people full of God's love, awakening to intimacy with Him just like I have. They will see chains broken all over the world. Friend, you are a member of that army.

Soon after I turned my life over to Christ, I received a prophetic word at XA's large group meeting. As I came down front for prayer, an elderly man who had visited that night grabbed my arm. I knelt down, and the man put his hand on my head. I listened as he loudly spoke in my ear in his prayer language. I was a little intimidated—OK, very intimidated—but super intrigued. He was saying exactly what I needed to hear! He said that God would bring about a new beginning for me and that God was about to do a new thing in my life.

Later that night, I helped our campus pastor, Justin Felch, move all of our worship equipment back to his trailer. That night, Justin shared a verse with me: "See, I am doing a new thing! Now it springs up; do you not perceive it? I am making a way in the wilderness and streams in the wasteland" (Isa. 43:19). I almost wept as he described the new beginning that he believed God had for me. I asked him what he thought God would make new for me. He said he felt God saying, "Behold, I am making all things new." This word came to pass literally within a month. Within a few days, I got a new car. A few days later, I got a new and better job at Troy University. A few days after that, I met my wife, and we went out on a date for the first time.

On our first date, I saw on a sign at a nearby church that read, "It's time for a new beginning." For me, this was a huge confirmation that Jess was to be mine in marriage. In those days, I carried a disposable camera everywhere I went and took pictures of what I believed God was speaking to me. I stopped after I dropped Jess off at her house and took a picture of the sign. On the way home, I stopped and got gas. As I went in to pay, looking for God's voice, I noticed the headline for the paper that day: "A new day has dawned."

God gives confirmation through all sorts of ways. Be open-minded and listen for His voice. He will certainly speak. Consider the book of

Job, which states, "For God speaks time and again, but a person may not notice it" (Job 33:14 HCSB). I encourage you to notice His voice and to eagerly look for it.

FORGIVENESS
It wasn't long before my parents found out about my past and all the wrong I had done. I will never forget that night, standing out in the yard with my mom. She looked at me and said, "Woody, I don't care what you've done. Jesus loves you, and I do, too. It's gone, sweet baby."

I was so choked up, I couldn't say much. That moment changed my life more than she knew. Because of her, I felt reassured that God wasn't angry with me, as I had wondered at times. Maybe, just maybe, God was waiting for me to come home all along, just like she was. Through this moment, God continued to draw me into the secret place.

You see, the journey to the secret place is as intentional as it is unintentional. Despite your efforts and against your own will, God will continue to romance you. Most of the time, these romantic moments can be so subtle, so *normal*, that we may never give Him credit for them. I don't think He minds if you know He is romancing you or not. He simply wants your heart, no matter who gets the credit for it. This chapter and the previous one chronical many of those unintentional happenings that drew me to Him. I hope that through them you can notice your own, sometimes covert, *Jehovah-sneaky* God-romance moments and surrender your life to the secret place.

YOUR FIRST STEP
I often wondered if I needed Jesus more than most people. I certainly felt that way. Maybe you feel messed up, too. I invite you to take the first intentional step into the secret place with God. Give your heart to Him. Take a moment, and in your own words, ask Him to forgive your sin. Ask Him to come into your heart and life and change you from the inside out. Ask Him to begin a relationship with you. He will.

I have included some foundational material in the appendix of this book that is essential for the new believer to grasp. In it, I discuss the attributes of God, God's relationship with the believer, how to properly be led by the Lord, fasting, reverence, and genuine humility. Through this foundational material, I hope to give you a solid theological base to build a relationship with Christ that lasts through your entire life.

If you just invited Christ in your heart, then I would like to hear your story. My website and social media information is located at the back of this book.

4

The Secret Place

What's the secret to real freedom that I searched desperately for in the boxes I spoke of in the preface? What eventually set me free from my insecure unbalanced destructive life I spoke of in chapter 1? What set me free from the shame, guilt, depression, and addiction that I spoke of in chapters 2 and 3? The answer is not a system, program, or a pill. Simply put, the answer is an introduction and an intentionally sustained relationship with God. When you find the one your soul longs for (Christ) and you cultivate that relationship, you will find wholeness, freedom, and real life. In John 10:10 NLT, Christ Himself says, "My purpose is to give them a rich and satisfying life."

This chapter is the beginning of our journey into the secret place of intimacy with God. I would love to be your guide, if you will have me. Let's begin.

ELYON

If I were to ask you your name in English, you would tell me your title, what people call you. But if I were Hebrew and I asked you your name, you would tell me three things:

1. Who you are, or the name people call you
2. What you are like
3. What you have done

In the Hebrew language, for every characteristic of God, there is a specific name that describes Him based on the three things above. The names are different depending on what characterizes Him in the context of the moment. It's actually astounding to look at the number of names used to describe God in the Bible. For this book, I want to focus on one name attributed to God—Elyon.

In Hebrew, *Elyon* means *uppermost* or *highest*. It means the top in altitude of something, not necessarily of a government structure, but of elevation. For example, the Elyon of a pine tree is the pine needles at the very tip-top of the tree. This name for God is used for when His location matters to the story.

Let's look at three scriptures:

1. "Fixing our eyes on Jesus, the Pioneer and Perfecter of faith. For the joy set before Him He endured the cross, scorning its shame, and sat down at the *right hand* of the throne of God" (Heb. 12:2, emphasis mine).
2. "You make known to me the path of life; You will fill me with joy in Your presence, with eternal pleasures at Your *right hand*" (Ps. 16:11, emphasis mine).
3. "And *God raised us up with Christ and seated us with Him in the heavenly realms* in Christ Jesus, in order that in the coming ages He might show the incomparable riches of His grace, expressed in His kindness to us in Christ Jesus" (Eph. 2:6–7, emphasis mine).

If God is in Elyon and Christ has been raised to where He is, then Christ has been raised to Elyon—at God's right hand. Psalm 16:11 says that in God's right hand are pleasures forever more. This means that in Elyon, where Christ is seated, are pleasures forever more.

Ephesians 2:6 says that you have been seated with Christ. Christ, remember, is seated in Elyon. As strange as it may sound, you are supernaturally, at this very moment, in two places at once. You are seated with

Christ in heaven, at the source of all pleasure, as well as seated on earth. Let's dig a little deeper into scripture and figure out why.

First, let's take a quick look at Psalm 91:1–2 NJB: "You who live in the secret place of *Elyon*, spend your nights in the shelter of *Shaddai*, saying to *Yahweh*, 'My refuge, my fortress, my *God* in whom I trust!'" In this verse are four names for God. For our purposes I want to define them for you. From my studies in scripture, these are the simplest definitions for them.

1. Elyon: the Highest
2. Shaddai: the Almighty, or the Strongest
3. Yahweh: Holy and Sacred name for God
4. God (Elohim): the Creator

Let's read those verses again with my emphasis replacing the names of God for their rough definitions: You who live in the secret place of the *Highest*, spend your nights in the shelter of *the Strongest*, saying to *the Holy and Sacred One*, My refuge, my fortress, *my Creator* in whom I trust!"

These first two verses are a condition for the rest of the Psalm. It is reserving the rest of the chapter for those who abide by the condition in the first two verses. Those conditions are

1. You who live in the secret place of the Highest,
2. You who spend your nights in the shelter of the Strongest, and
3. You who say to the Holy and Sacred One, my refuge, my fortress, my Creator in whom I trust.

In the verses, God is specifically addressing those who live in the secret place. I had the same questions as you probably do now: "How do I dwell in the secret place? How do I dwell in the shelter of the Strongest? What does that mean?" For the answer, let's look to the Bible once again:

If you have been raised with Christ [to a new life, thus sharing His resurrection from the dead], aim at and seek the [rich, eternal treasures] that are above, where Christ is, seated at the right hand of God. And set your minds and keep them set on what is above (the higher things), not on the things that are on the earth. For [as much as this world is concerned] you have died, and your [new, real] life is hidden with Christ in God. (Col. 3:1–4 AMP)

The answer is found in three things outlined in the following verse.

1. If you have been raised with Christ, *you must be born again.*
2. Aim at and seek the [rich, eternal treasures] that are above, where Christ, seated at the right hand of God.
3. Set your minds and keep them set on what is above (the higher things), not on the things that are on the earth.

I aim and set my mind by spending quality time with Jesus every single day. I worship, pray, and read my Bible—a lot. In doing that, I can stay in interaction with Him all day long. I will go into a lot of details about this in the next six chapters.

If you live in the secret place, let's look back at Psalm 91 NJB in detail and see what will happen. The benefits of the secret place are:

1. No traps (verse 3): "He rescues you from the snare of the fowler set on destruction."
2. Protection (verse 4): "He covers you with His pinions, you find shelter under His wings. His constancy is shield and protection."
3. No fear and protection from evil people (verse 5): "You need not fear the terrors of night, the arrow that flies in the daytime,"
4. No fear and protection from disease (verse 6): "The plague that stalks in the darkness, the scourge that wreaks havoc at high noon."
5. No fear and protection in battle (verse 7):"Though a thousand fall at your side, ten thousand at your right hand, you yourself will remain unscathed."

6. You will have insight, and you will see the evil repaid by the wicked (verses 8 and 9): "You have only to keep your eyes open to see how the wicked are repaid, you who say, 'Yahweh my refuge!' and make Elyon your fortress."
7. No disaster or widespread disease can be victorious over you (verses 9 and 10): "No disaster can overtake you, no plague come near your tent;"
8. Angels guard you (verse 11): "He has given his angels orders about you to guard you wherever you go."
9. Angels also catch you if you stumble, and they also carry you in the hard times of life (verse 12): "They will carry you in their arms in case you trip over a stone."
10. You trample down your enemies and those who would oppose you without being harmed (verse 13): "You will walk upon wild beast and adder, you will trample young lions and snakes."
11. Because you hold tight to the Lord, you are raised high, a place of protection from all foes (verse 14): "Since he clings to me I rescue him, I raise him high, since he acknowledges my name."
12. God promises to answer your prayers and be by your side through any hard time, and He also promises to rescue you and bring you honor (verse 15): "He calls to me and I answer him: in distress I am at his side, I rescue him and bring him honour."
13. Long life and Salvation (verse 16): "I shall satisfy him with long life, and grant him to see my salvation."

TURNING POINT

I don't cry myself to sleep in shame and hurt anymore. I'm not bound up by pornography, random sex, or unled ministry works anymore. I'm freer than I ever could have imagined because of my intimacy with God. The secret place of His love saved my marriage and my life.

During my time in student ministry, I have unofficially quit several times. The root of this I would assume is fear. I used to walk in fear, which would lead to depression, which would lead back to fear. This depression stuff would wave over me, which in turn would lead to sin. Also, during my time in street ministry I used to fear…a lot. When you're walking up to a brothel, a crack house, a homeless shelter, or an abandoned building to tell people about Jesus, there can be a lot going on in your mind. A lot of fear can build up. A while back, a gangbanging thief in a neighborhood I go to stopped me for prayer. He said, "Don't be nervous." I said, "OK!" In my heart, I was wetting my pants!

Because I am living in the secret place, when I go out now I have balance and I don't have fear. Fear simply doesn't exist. I know deep down that I should have fear. But I just can't produce the feeling. Traps and addictions are gone. I am free.

JOHN 14:12

Why would God raise us to Elyon, the secret place, and have us still on the earth? Because He has created a fearless, protected, super soldier for the kingdom of heaven. You are heaven's ambassadors to the earth. Having been raised with Him, we have become citizens of heaven and placed in a seat of authority. Why? You're part of God's plan to take this planet to destroy the works of the devil. You are fulfilling the Lord's Prayer: "Your kingdom come, Your will be done, on earth as it is in heaven."

In John 14:12, Jesus says you're going do the works you've seen Him do, plus you're going do greater because He goes to the Father. God is the ultimate strategist. The hidden secret was, He was taking you with Him to the Father! To Elyon! To a position of authority!

It is the will of God that the will of heaven be established on the earth. You as a coheir with Christ, full of the Holy Spirit and dwelling in Elyon, are a force to be reckoned with!

TIME TO HAVE SOME FUN

In the next six chapters, we will discover six different parts of the secret place and some fun stories of how God and I have spent time in each. These six places are:

1. Freedom from Junk
2. Meditation

3. Face to Face
4. Marriage with Christ
5. The Fountain of Life
6. Overflow

The parts of the secret place I describe in this book are only a practical tool to help you begin your intimacy with God. The last thing I want to do is make you believe that these six parts are the only way to be intimate with God. Intimacy with God is not a formula—it is a relationship. The only thing that determines the boundaries of a relationship with Christ is the Bible.

How could any book contain the fullness of the marriage relationship between you and your Creator? I'm positive that I don't know everything about this subject, and I'm not sure that anyone ever will. However, what I have enjoyed and learned in the secret place I would love to share with you.

This is going to be a blast! I invite you to take your time and enjoy yourself during the rest of our time together.

5

Into the Secret Place, Part 1: Freedom from Junk

There once lived a guy who loved rocks. He collected them, looked at them, set them in observance in his house, and put them in his garden. However, his wife hated them—so much, in fact, that she would often take some of them while he was sleeping and throw them into the driveway just to get rid of a few. One summer day, he went camping. He decided to take a five-mile hike through the forested mountains to see the scenery and catch some fresh air. Along the way he began to pick up rocks—a few here and a few there. He quickly stuffed them into his backpack and continued hiking. The pack got heavier and heavier as he went along. Eventually, he had to empty the rocks out of his backpack just to make it back to the campsite.

Just like this guy with his rocks, we often carry things we can't see but can certainly feel the weight of. We carry our job pressures, worries, depression, anger, bitterness, rage, doubt, guilt, etc. There are a number of things we carry that should be laid down before the Lord. If we don't get rid of these "rocks" in our lives, they could cost us time and even cost us our lives or the lives of others. With all this extra stuff rushing through your mind, it becomes hard to hear what God is saying and what He wants for your life. It becomes difficult to interact with Him. In this chapter, you will learn a simple model that will hopefully help you learn how to lay this stuff down, just as the man who loved rocks did by emptying his backpack.

Before we discuss a method—though not the only method—of removing stones from our pack, let's discuss the stones themselves. In this chapter, I will identify four main stones that we all tend to pick up along the way.

STONE #1: GUILT

It is highly necessary that I cover the difference between *guilt* and *conviction* here. If I waited to cover it in one of the later chapters, chances are you would never make it past this one, because guilt kills your prayer life. Guilt makes you ashamed to approach Christ and His throne of grace. The Bible says, "So let us come boldly to the throne of our gracious God. There we will receive His mercy, and we will find grace to help us when we need it most" (Heb. 4:16 NLT). Conviction, however, makes your prayer life grow by leaps and bounds. Conviction is the gentle push of a loving Father away from things that will harm you. In order to move forward, it is important to know the difference between the two. Let's discuss them in detail.

In order to understand the difference between guilt and conviction, it's important to first understand certain aspects of your salvation. When you became a Christian, along with your sins being washed away in the blood of Jesus, a few other awesome supernatural things happened to you. One of those supernatural happenings is that you became a brand-new creation. "Therefore if any man be in Christ, he is a new creature: old things are passed away; behold, all things are become new" (2 Cor. 5:17 KJV). (Also see John 1:13; Rom. 6:4; Gal. 6:15)

The Bible actually uses the Greek word *kainoj*—pronounced "kahee-nos"—for the word *new* in 2 Corinthians 5:17. *Kainoj* means "new in freshness; recently made fresh, recent, unused, unworn; *of a new kind, unprecedented*, novel, uncommon, *unheard of*" (Strong's Concordance #G2537, emphasis mine). In other instances, the word used for *new* in the Bible translates as *neoj* in the Greek. *Neoj* is pronounced "neh'-os" and means "recently born, young, youthful" (Strong's Concordance #G3501). What I need you to notice is the difference between the two words *kainoj* and *neoj*. They both mean "new" in English, but in Greek they mean so much more. When you came to Christ, you were made not just new (*neoj*),

36

but you were made *kainoj* ("new and unprecedented; unheard of")! God didn't just wash you off—He made you totally new! You are a new and better creation than the one you once were, one the likes of the earth has never seen before.

Along with this new you, you were given a new nature, much different than the sinful nature you were born with: "For I was born a sinner—yes, from the moment my mother conceived me" (Ps. 51:5 NLT). Now that you have been "reborn" as a new *kainoj* creation, the Bible refers to this as bringing you to life.

> And you who were dead in trespasses and in the uncircumcision of your flesh (your sensuality, your sinful carnal nature), [God] brought to life together with [Christ], having [freely] forgiven us all our transgressions, having cancelled and blotted out and wiped away the handwriting of the note (bond) with its legal decrees and demands which was in force and stood against us (hostile to us). This [note with its regulations, decrees, and demands] He set aside and cleared completely out of our way by nailing it to [His] cross. [God] disarmed the principalities and powers that were ranged against us and made a bold display and public example of them, in triumphing over them in Him and in it [the cross]. (Col. 2:13–15 AMP)

The Bible also refers to your new *kainoj* identity as a "saint," not a "sinner." Your sinful nature has been crucified with Christ! It is gone! "Those who belong to Christ Jesus have nailed the passions and desires of their sinful nature to His cross and crucified them there" (Gal. 5:24–26 NLT). Paul the apostle also makes this apparent in many of his books in the New Testament. Consider, for example, what he says in Ephesians when he addresses the entire book to the saints at Ephesus: "Paul, an apostle of Jesus Christ by the will of God, to the saints who are in Ephesus, and are faithful in Christ Jesus" (Eph. 1:1 ESV). Consider also, for example, Paul's address to the Colossians: "To the saints and faithful brethren in Christ which are at Colosse: Grace *be* unto you, and peace, from God our Father and the Lord Jesus Christ" (Col. 1:2 KJV). The reality is that you have a new nature with new Godly direction and desires—the nature of a *saint*. This new nature can be thought of this way: the *natural* thing for you now is *to not sin*, whereas the *natural* thing for you to do before *was to sin*.

This new nature is a byproduct of now having the Holy Spirit living inside you. You literally now naturally love what the Holy Spirit loves and naturally hate what the Holy Spirit hates. When you sin, you "grieve" the Holy Spirit that's living inside you. "And do not grieve the Holy Spirit of God, with Whom you were sealed for the day of redemption" (Eph. 4:30). Sin grieves Him. This causes discomfort in your heart, because He feels discomforted by sin. Because He is inside you, you are now feeling what He feels and thinking what He thinks. "For who has known or understood the mind (the counsels and purposes) of the Lord so as to guide and instruct Him and give Him knowledge? But we have the mind of Christ (the Messiah) and do hold the thoughts (feeling and purposes) of His heart" (1 Cor. 2:16 AMP).

This means a lot for us as Christians, but for the purpose of understanding the difference between guilt and conviction, it means that you will feel and know the negativity that the Holy Spirit feels and thinks about an action of sin. The bad feeling due to sin is known as conviction. It is your built-in warning system letting you know when you're doing something that will ruin your life. It's similar to that beeping noise you hear that lets you know that you don't have your seatbelt on while riding in your car. It is there to protect you from hurting yourself and those around you. Many times I can feel the Holy Spirit warning me of possible traps of sin that have been laid for me. It's when I follow His lead that I am able to walk in freedom. When I refuse His guidance in conviction, I become trapped. My natural tendency now as a saint is to follow my loving Father away from sin.

While conviction is a process that leads to spiritual life and repentance of sin, "guilt" is a process that leads to shame and spiritual death. Guilt is very sneaky. It usually comes very close after conviction and can last for days, years, or even a lifetime. A good way to tell the difference be-tween conviction and guilt is that conviction will leave after a sin has been repented—after you have turned away from sin and changed your mind about that sin. If you are living in pain over something you have repented for, chances are you are feeling guilt and not conviction.

Conviction is not there to shame you; it is there to lead you down the right path that is best for your life. We can see a perfect model of this in the Bible:

At dawn He appeared again in the temple courts, where all the people gathered around Him, and He sat down to teach them. The teachers of the law and the Pharisees brought in a woman caught in adultery. They made her stand before the group and said to Jesus, "Teacher, this woman was caught in the act of adultery. In the Law Moses commanded us to stone such women. Now what do You say?" They were using this question as a trap, in order to have a basis for accusing Him.

But Jesus bent down and started to write on the ground with His finger. When they kept on questioning Him, He straightened up and said to them, "Let any one of you who is without sin be the first to throw a stone at her." Again He stooped down and wrote on the ground.

At this, those who heard began to go away one at a time, the older ones first, until only Jesus was left, with the woman still standing there. Jesus straightened up and asked her, "Woman, where are they? Has no one condemned you?"

"No one, sir," she said.

"Then neither do I condemn you," Jesus declared. "Go now and leave your life of sin." (John 8:2–11)

Jesus simply saved her life and ripped shame off of her. The religious leaders were ready to put her to shame and death. However, Jesus did not condemn her like these religious folk of the day. Instead, He lifted her up off the ground and gave her direction for her life. This is the true difference between conviction and guilt. Conviction gives correction with direction. Guilt gives shame and spiritual death.

If you are struggling with guilt, please know that God has taken your sin and blotted it out forever. He has removed it as far as the east from the west (Ps. 103:12). Jesus will never leave you nor forsake you (Deut. 31:6–8; Heb. 13:5; Josh. 1:9)—but when you put your faith in your works to be righteous instead of putting your faith in Christ's work that made you righteous, you will live in guilt. You might think He somehow wants you to work off your sin to right the wrong. The truth is that you could never undo the wrong—that's why He came! He righted the wrong two thousand years ago when He died in your place, taking your punishment for that sin. "God made Him who had no sin to be sin for us, so that in Him we might become the righteousness of God" (2 Cor. 5:21).

You, right now, are the righteousness of God! You are the holiest thing on planet Earth because of Him. Salvation is believing and accepting Christ's righteousness over your own. It's believing, accepting, and relying on the fact that He died in your place, living the perfect, mistake-free life you could never live. Believe in what He has done for you, not what you have done—good or bad! Believing in your sin, or lack of righteousness, and not in Christ actually empowers those things to ruin your life through guilt.

STONE #2: SIN

The primary door to guilt is sin. When you do sin (which is an intentional act that is contrary to the perfect will of God), identify the Holy Spirit's conviction, repent, and move on. You are not a complete failure, and you are not totally useless to God, even though you may feel like it in the moment of sin. Even though Christ was sinless, He was tempted. Consider the verse:

> For we do not have a high priest who is unable to empathize with our weaknesses, but we have one who has been tempted

in every way, just as we are—yet he did not sin. Let us then approach God's throne of grace with confidence, so that we may receive mercy and find grace to help us in our time of need. (Heb. 4:15–16)

Christ identifies with you and draws you back to the light. Christ, the Bible says, is our "advocate" with the Father. He claims us despite any of our momentary failures. He said:

My little children, I am writing these things to you so that you may not sin. But if anyone does sin, we have an advocate with the Father, Jesus Christ the righteous. He is the propitiation for our sins, and not for ours only but also for the sins of the whole world. (1 John 2:1–2 ESV)

Also realize that you are still considered a saint despite an occasional sin. As a saint, it is not in your nature to sin, although it may happen from time to time. Like a fish out of water are you to sin. It is not something that you were created to thrive in. Sinning is not something that you naturally agree with, or you wouldn't have felt conviction about it. My advice is to confess it to Christ, move on, and forgive yourself as Christ has forgiven you. "If we confess our sins, He is faithful and just and will forgive us our sins and purify us from all unrighteousness" (1 John 1:9).

Don't depend on your own righteousness for your relationship with God; depend on Christ's righteousness. Don't be like the guys who said, "'Lord, Lord, did we not prophesy in Your name and in Your name drive out demons and in Your name perform many miracles?' *Then the Lord replies,* Then I will tell them plainly, 'I never knew you, away from Me, you evildoers!'" (Matt. 7:22–23, emphasis mine). The problem here is that they depended on their own good deeds for salvation. The reality is that it is just as bad to assume that your momentary sin would keep you from heaven as it is to assume that your good deeds would get you there. In both cases, your faith is in the wrong person.

Have faith in Christ, depending on His righteousness over your own. Repent (change the way you think about the act involved with the sin), and move on with your life. God has chosen not to remember it; by His grace and power you can, too. "I, I am He who blots out your transgressions for My own sake, and I will not remember your sins" (Isa. 43:25 ESV).

If you are involved in sin, guilt, or shame that you cannot shake, I encourage you to share it with trusted friends who love you or pastors you trust. The Bible says concerning this type of sin, "Therefore confess your sins to each other and pray for each other so that you may be healed. The prayer of a righteous person is powerful and effective" (James 5:15). The reality is that God designed you to be forgiven by Him and healed in a community of believers. Get in a community such as a small group, share your faults, get support, and be healed.

STONE #3: INNER AGREEMENTS/INNER VOWS

Have you ever been in a tough situation and said to yourself, "I'll never let that happen again!" or "I will never be like this person?" Of course you have—we all have. Unfortunately, thinking that way could keep you stuck in a rut just as much as guilt will. Let me give you an example.

Let's say you are a woman reading this and you have been abused by a man in the past—maybe even your father or someone you looked up to. When you were abused, you either said out loud or in your heart, "I will NEVER let a man hurt me like that again." The good thing about that thought process ("I will NEVER...") at the time of the abuse is that you probably fought back and hopefully got out of the relationship somehow. You may have stayed away from the man—and stayed true to the inner agreement made—by saying, "I will NEVER let that happen again," which protected you from being hurt again by him.

The problem arises when later in life you are engaged with a truly loving man. That inner agreement begins to work against you instead of for you. You begin to distance yourself from the loving man because of it. It is likely that you are unaware of your inner agreement. You may even wonder why you act that way around men. The problem is that when you said, "I will NEVER let this happen again," you spiritually built a wall to protect yourself from men. Unfortunately, that wall is not discriminatory. It doesn't pick and choose who it keeps out of your heart. Sometimes those walls can even keep us from a loving relationship with Christ. It creates a stronghold.

There are many situations where I have made inner agreements with myself and have said, either out loud or in my heart, "I will NEVER let that happen again." The example of the woman in the hypothetical story above is just one of many that I have seen in my time in ministry. I've also seen people who tragically believe that just because they say, "I'll never be like them," or "I'll never do that," they end up getting propelled toward the very thing that they don't want to do. I've found that my relationship with Christ can move forward when I tear down the walls that keep Him out of certain hurt places in my heart and trust Him in everything.

Instead of saying, "I will NEVER let that happen again," let's give those inner agreements to Christ and let Him make sure it doesn't happen again. In a spiritual war, sometimes we get attacked out of nowhere. Building a wall in your heart will only make things worse for you. Let's trust in the person of Christ.

Inner agreements can be made because of almost any negative situation you can think of. Inner agreements do not all have to begin with "I will never." There are all sorts of ways these can come about. Take a moment, and ask God to reveal any inner agreements you may have made. Chances are that there are several, just as there were in my own life.

I want to encourage you that if something illegal is happening to you, get the police involved. Holding these things in does not protect you or your perpetrator. It equips that person to do the same thing to others. Once the police have handled the situation, I encourage you to give that inner agreement to the Lord. I suggest giving it to God in the way I will describe at the end of this chapter.

Take as much time as you need. Renounce those inner agreements one by one. The more time you spend doing this, the more inner agreements God can remove from your life and the healthier Christian you will be.

STONE #4: MOURNING

I prefer the method of Enoch and Elijah, where they did not die but were taken (Heb. 11:5 and 2 Kings 2:1). However, when someone does die, mourn for a season—and after the season is over, give that mourning to God.

Mourning for the rest of your life will cause physical as well as spiritual rot. Years of mourning disguises itself as, "I just miss them," when in reality it can quickly lead to depression. Depression can lead to guilt, and guilt and depression can both lead to death. Many health problems are caused by mourning for extended periods.

Mourn for a moment, and celebrate that person's life for a lifetime. Find a way to honor and remember him or her that is positive. Maybe even write a nice book about that loved one! Whatever it is, do something positive for the world in remembrance. That's what God and that person would want you to do.

DON'T GET FRUSTRATED–BE HAPPY!

Hundreds of times a day, things happen that weigh us down. Giving those things to God will help you to live without that weight and prepare you for part two of the secret place. Try not to get frustrated if this takes a while. The time spent here will pay off. The freedom from junk you carry is worth it. This part of the secret place has gotten faster and faster with me each and every time. As God has dealt with the rocks in my life, the rocks became fewer and fewer to deal with on a regular basis.

Having now defined "rocks," let's discuss a prayer model to remove them from our packs.

FREEDOM PRAYER MODEL

Once you have the following model down, please experiment (biblically) with God concerning other ways you can go through this process of getting rid of the "rocks" in your heart (or mind). However, remember that God does it for you; allow Him to clean out your "backpack," or your mind and heart of "junk." The way He does this can and will likely change from time to time as seasons change in your life. It may even change daily! In no way will I ever say this is the only way God can or will clear your heart and mind of junk. Again, this is simply a model—a great place to start.

Step 1
Find a quiet spot that is free of distractions.

Step 2
Put on some worship music that is God-focused and positive—nothing about struggling or hurting. Here's a hint: don't listen to any music that connects you to your old life or your mistakes ("God is great!" type music). Bethel Music is one of my favorite bands. I encourage you to look it up.

Step 3
Close your eyes. Hold out your hands in front of you as if you're holding water that is scooped up into your hands. Ask God to reveal to you things that are hindrances, or "rocks," in your pack.

Step 4
Imagine (by faith) one by one those things that are weighing on your mind and heart in the palms of your hands. Here's a hint: turn negative feelings into something small that you can imagine in the palms of your hands. You may have many different negative feelings going on inside you at the same time. For starters, try only imagining and pinpointing one thing in your hands at a time. For example, if you're angry at someone, imagine that person or an object related to the anger in the cup of your hands. Then continue to the next step.

Step 5
Next, I want you to imagine (by faith) God's hand literally taking those things from your hands as if you are passing them to Him or as if He were taking them from you. Put whatever "rocks" God sends to your mind in the cup of your hands and hand them over to Him. One by one, as those

things come to your mind, ask God to take them from you, and imagine Him doing so.

Step 6

As He takes them from you, intentionally change your mind ("repent," believing what God says in His word about you and this situation), and you will feel them leave—anger, worry, pressure, doubt, depression, anxiety, fear, etc. You will be amazed at the peace you will have after praying in this way. Spend the next fifteen minutes praying in this manner.

Here's another hint: don't rush. The Holy Spirit is going to bring lots of things to your mind. Do not ignore the things He brings up to your thoughts, as they are most likely what He needs to deal with in your life at that moment. Stay here as long as you need to clear your mind, repent, and get centered on God.

As a personal example, I dealt with a ton of shame about something I did wrong. I sat down and closed my eyes. I imagined the shame as an object (in this case, a piece of paper) in my hands. As I watched, the Lord took what I had imagined was in my hands. He wadded it up and threw it in the trash. He then gave me a huge hug. I could feel the presence and love of the Father in that moment. I felt so refreshed and so at peace.

Keep your heart open. God may do this same thing a little different in your own way. I have a buddy who took a small group out and exploded with dynamite the issues that the group had written on pieces of paper. By doing so, he was giving them to God. I have been in a service where almost five hundred people nailed personal issues written on paper to a big wooden cross. I have been in a small group service where we burned issues written on paper in a bonfire. I have personally written my issues down on paper and burned them in my fireplace. However you find success in giving stuff to God by faith, go for it.

When using your imagination (by faith) as a communication tool, remember that God will never say or do anything contrary to His word. When you feel that God is saying something to you, *always* run it by the

Bible first. If what you hear or see contradicts written scripture, it wasn't God. We will talk about this more in the next chapter.

MINISTRY APPLICATION

As a pastor and teacher of the word, this model is a critical part of my life. It is a great way to get those little things that bug me out of my mind so that I can focus on hearing from the Lord and ministering His heart. This is also a unique way to give intercession back to the Lord. Intercession, in its simplest definition, is praying for people. Being an intercessor means that you pray for people often. Many times when you're praying for a family member or a situation in your life, it's easy to slip into a life of depression or anxiety before you realize it. In order to be a healthy, happy intercessor, you must learn to lay that thing you're interceding for down once you've finished praying.

Please remember that this is only a model. Feel free to put your own spin on things and to change it as you want! As God leads you, you are free to be you. God created us all differently—from our fingerprints and personalities to the way we worship and the way we pray. Please experiment, in a biblical way, with other ways that God can clean the junk out of your "backpack." However He does it, make sure He does so, so that you can walk into a greater intimacy with Him.

6

Into the Secret Place, Part 2: Meditation

Welcome to our second part of the secret place. In this part of the secret place, your thoughts are pointed to God. Thinking about God is simply known as *meditation*. There are many examples of meditation prayers in the Bible. One of my favorites is Psalm 23. The writer, King David, often spent time meditating and singing songs to God. As David sings this song, he ponders line by line what each sentence means in his heart.

> The Lord is my shepherd, I lack nothing.
> He makes me lie down in green pastures, He leads me beside quiet waters, He refreshes my soul.
> He guides me along the right paths for His name's sake.
> Even though I walk through the darkest valley, I will fear no evil, for You are with me; Your rod and Your staff, they comfort me.
> You prepare a table before me in the presence of my enemies.
> You anoint my head with oil; my cup overflows.
> Surely Your goodness and love will follow me all the days of my life, and I will dwell in the house of the Lord forever.

I am convinced that this type of meditation is one way that David celebrated an intimacy with the Lord. "After removing Saul, He made David their king. God testified concerning him: 'I have found David son of

Jesse, a man after My own heart; he will do everything I want him to do.'" (Acts 13:22).

LINKING MEDITATION AND WORSHIP

Take a moment and think of how worship songs are composed. They often repeat the same phrases over and over. Consider Hillsong United's song, which simply says, "There is no one like You," repeating twenty or thirty times. Consider also the song "Halleluiah" by the same group, which states over and over many times, "Halleluiah, Our God Reigns."

Consider Hillsong United's song "Shout unto God," which repeats the following over and over:

The enemy has been defeated,
And death couldn't hold You down,
We're going to lift our voice in victory,
Going to make our praises loud.
Shout unto God with a voice of Triumph,
Shout unto God with a voice of Praise,
Shout unto God with a voice of Triumph,
We lift Your name up,
We lift Your name up

Take a moment and think of every worship song that you can imagine. It is likely that most or part of the song is repeated over and over. This musical model of repetition is very helpful in pointing your thoughts to God and focusing on Him. As you meditate and worship to these repetitive songs, ponder what the words mean to you.

I encourage you to feast on music and media that focuses on God and positivity—not your problems, worries, fears, or anxieties. Meditating on your problems will only make them seem bigger and likely will make things worse. "Finally, brothers and sisters, whatever is true, whatever is noble, whatever is right, whatever is pure, whatever is lovely, whatever is admirable—if anything is excellent or praiseworthy—think about such things" (Phil. 4:8).

During meditation on God, you may feel like singing, shouting, painting, or dancing—and I encourage you to do so. Whatever you want to do with God, I encourage you to do. As you sing, pray, dance, paint, write, read, play—whatever you're doing—intentionally have your thoughts on Him.

Eventually your thoughts will begin to always remain on Him with little effort, even when you aren't in a time devoted specifically to it. Believe it or not, you will actually find it more difficult not to have your thoughts on Him. I am now able to work, drive, play, etc., and still remain in this meditative state. My thoughts are constantly on God no matter what I am doing. I love living in a constant state of prayer, whether I'm hiking, eating dinner with friends, or at work. As my beautiful wife puts it: Godly meditation is "praying without ceasing" or "praying continually." "Rejoice always, pray without ceasing, in everything give thanks; for this is the will of God in Christ Jesus for you" (1 Thess. 5:16–18 KJV).

PRAY BEYOND YOUR BREAKTHROUGH!
I encourage you to rethink the adage, "Pray until you feel a breakthrough." Have you ever heard anyone say that? The thought is that you should pray until you feel peace. When God brings you peace from your "rocks" or "junk," I actually encourage you to keep on praying and meditating. If you do, you will reach new places in prayer. You will begin to experience what I believe are the "heavenly things" that Jesus speaks of in John 3:12. "I have spoken to you of earthly things and you do not believe; how then will you believe if I speak of heavenly things?" (John 3:12). Here you will begin to experience the presence of God, visions, and other heavenly experiences—although it is possible that you have already experienced them.

USE YOUR IMAGINATION!
In the last chapter, we briefly discussed your imagination and what God uses it for. I want to take a minute and elaborate on that topic. First, consider this: you were created to be in relationship with God. Everything about you, a

created being, was created to communicate and interact with your Heavenly Creator—God. Chances are, you have interacted with God much more than you realize. Remember that much of interacting with God is by faith.

When you close your eyes, you see nothing but the color black. Think of the black you see with your eyes closed as God's blackboard: a place for Him to write and draw. Not all things that get drawn and seen on that chalkboard are from God, but all the good things are. Remember the verse: "Whatever is good and perfect is a gift coming down to us from God our Father, who created all the lights in the heavens. He never changes or casts a shifting shadow" (James 1:17 NLT). This verse includes your good thoughts.

I encourage you during the upcoming prayer model to simply let your mind run wild with thoughts of interaction with Him. By faith in the secret place, I pray you will awaken to visions, heavenly realities, and experiences. God and I have walked throughout heaven, danced in fields, walked through a palace, looked at kingdoms, and even sat around a campfire. Our interactions have been very basic, like I just described, or very complex. My favorite interactions with God, however, are the ones that a typical father and son enjoy together, from playing catch to watching stars together in a field.

One night, when God healed me of a serious inward struggle, I, by faith, sat on His shoulders by the beach. I remember from that experience that He was so big in that moment. I needed freedom from fear, and that is what He gave me. There is no limit to the interactions to be had. I encourage you to experiment with this within biblical bounds as I have. You will be amazed at the things you can do and how much fun you can have with God. You are free right now to be yourself with your Daddy, God. "Now the Lord is the Spirit, and where the Spirit of the Lord is, there is freedom" (2 Cor. 3:17).

PROPHETIC EXPERIENCES

A person is considered a prophet when he or she has the specific gift of prophecy from the Holy Spirit. We all can prophesy, to speak God's heart, to a degree, but there is also a specific gift of prophecy that you can have if you ask the Holy Spirit for it. So often when people receive prophetic information from God in meditation, they stop praying.

Friend, the heart of prayer is relationship and intimacy with Him. When you find yourself going through a vision or other prophetic experience, I encourage you to not focus so heavily on the details around you. Instead, focus on God. Sometimes I know it can be a huge shock to be in a vision or to have a prophetic experience. Try to remain calm and not worry about having to remember everything. God doesn't care if you remember what you see enough to write it down as much as He just wants to spend some time with you. The overall point of the vision or experience is to bring you into a deeper intimacy with Him. Even more simply, He wants you to have fun with Him. If you choose to focus on the vision instead of God, you will likely come out of the experience before it's over. If God wants you to remember the vision, prophetic word, or other experience, then you will.

MEDITATION PRAYER MODEL
Here we will combine what we learned in the previous chapter with what we learned in this one. My hope for you in doing so is that you will go a little deeper in your interaction with God. Get excited! Let's go for it!

Step 1
Find a quiet spot that is free of distractions.

Step 2
Turn on some worship music that is God-focused and positive, just like we discussed a few pages back. (See Phil. 4:8)

Step 3
For starters, spend ten minutes letting your mind run with thoughts of God. I encourage you to meditate on the song that is playing. Begin to let God draw on your chalkboard like we discussed earlier.

The first time doing this should take about twenty minutes, so set up a worship playlist that is around twenty-five minutes long. Remember that God will be intimate with you when you engage Him in intimacy. "Come close to God, and God will come close to you" (James 4:8 NLT). I encourage you to talk *with* Him, not *at* Him, as you meditate on Him and share with Him your heart.

7

Into the Secret Place, Part 3: Face to Face

We are way more connected to the supernatural than we realize. We are, in fact, a spirit temporarily located in a human body, which also contains God's Spirit. Unfortunately, we aren't always conscious and aware of how connected we are to that realm. Nevertheless, we are forever locked in a face-to-face encounter with God, angels, and demons. When someone says they "encountered" something supernatural, they usually mean they saw, felt, heard, or smelled something that they couldn't quite understand. (God smells great, by the way.)

I would like to devote the next niche of the secret place to the presence of God and "encountering" the supernatural. In this chapter, I will share a few stories from my own experience face to face with God, angels, and demons. I hope to inspire you to love His presence and interacting with Him. Let's begin.

THE PRESENCE AND CLOSENESS OF GOD

First, let's discuss the relationship between the *presence* of God and the *closeness* of God. When discussing how close God is to you, it is important to understand the use of the word *close*. There are two ways to use this word: *close* as in "proximity" and *close* as in "intimacy."

As a child, when I was in class and the teacher called my name, I always answered with "Present!" This reply let the teacher know that I was in the room. As a Christian, you are as *close in proximity* to God right now as you will ever be. For starters, you have been raised with Christ to Elyon.

Second, Christ is present inside you—literally under your skin. Consider the verse: "For God wanted them to know that the riches and glory of Christ are for you Gentiles, too. And this is the secret: Christ lives in you. This gives you assurance of sharing his glory" (Col. 1:27 NLT). You will never and can never get any closer in proximity to Him. Christ lives inside your body, and simultaneously you are seated in heaven with Him.

In the first few years of my marriage, Jess was in a lot of emotional pain due to my neglect. She wanted me to get *closer* to her. You can understand that she did not mean closer as in proximity but closer as in intimacy. In the book of James, God says, "If you will come close to me I will come close to you" (James 4:8, paraphrase). In this verse, God wants the same thing that my wife wanted. He wants you to come close to Him intimately. It is then that He has promised to come close to you in intimacy. In James 4:8, God did not promise, "If you beg Me to come, I will." The promise was, "When you engage Me in intimacy, I will in turn engage you in intimacy."

Friend, be very careful not to shift the blame of a dry Christian experience to a worship leader, song selection, demonic spirit, or God. If you keep your end of the bargain—as you are learning how to do so—He will keep His promise to be intimate with you.

Consider the song "Let it Rain" by Michael W. Smith. The words ask God to "Let it rain / Open the floodgates of Heaven / Let it rain." What I want you to realize is that heaven was once and for all opened through Christ's cross and resurrection. Consider the scripture: "At that moment the curtain of the temple was torn in two from top to bottom. The earth shook, the rocks split" (Matt. 27:5). In this scripture, the partition from the Holy of Holies in the Temple, where God was, and the rest of the world was forever removed by Christ. In Acts 2, we can also see the moment when Christ sent the promised Holy Spirit to live in our bodies. Let's take a look.

When the day of Pentecost came, they were all together in one place. Suddenly a sound like the blowing of a violent wind came from heaven and filled the whole house where they were sitting. They saw what seemed to be tongues of fire that separated and came to rest on each of them. All of them were filled with the Holy Spirit and began to speak in other tongues as the Spirit enabled them. (Acts 2:1–4)

The Bible also shows us that in Christ we have the fullness of the Godhead and the kingdom of heaven inside us (Col. 2:9–10 and Luke 17:21 KJV). The reality is that through Christ we have become the "floodgates" of heaven. Instead of begging God to come down—which He did—look now for an invasion of God to the rest of the world springing out of you! If we are to see God's will be done around us, we must let God's kingdom "flood" out of us.

The only way to let God flood out of you into the rest of the world is to simply fall in love with Jesus, be intimate with Him, and do whatever overflows out of that love. Out of that secret place with God, you naturally will love people and follow your destiny. Being intimate with the Lord may seem like a waste of time to some religious folk, but it is the very thing you were created for and the key to your destiny. "Take delight in the Lord, and he will give you the desires of your heart. Commit your way to the Lord; trust in Him and He will do this: He will make your righteous reward shine like the dawn, your vindication like the noonday sun" (Ps. 37:4–6). "The Lord makes firm the steps of the one who delights in Him" (Ps. 37:23). (Also see Mark 12:30–31)

Sadly, some Christians seem as though they are stuck one day before Pentecost (Acts 2)—always pleading for God to come down and for His Spirit to "show up." When Christians beg God to come like this, it portrays God as distant and hard to reach. By their own erroneous faith, they believe that He is not already in the room, and they are therefore waiting on someone who's already arrived.

I once ordered a CD online and waited for it to come in the mail. Months went by, and the CD had not arrived. Every day I checked the mail. One day I decided to go through the junk mail on the kitchen table and found the CD! Had I continued to wait on something to arrive that had already arrived, I would have missed the CD entirely. Unfortunately, I think this happens all the time in some churches.

Let us awaken to the reality right now that God was reached once and for all by Christ on our behalf. Let's spend all of our worship and prayer time celebrating that He is here and not waste another minute begging for something to happen that has already taken place. You and God are now inseparable. When you show up, God shows up. "Do you not know that your bodies are temples of the Holy Spirit, Who is in you, Whom you have received from God? You are not your own" (1 Cor. 6:19). "Neither shall they say, Lo here! or, lo there! For, behold, the kingdom of God is within you" (Luke 17:21 KJV). He is not somewhere out in the distance, just far enough to not get offended by you. The Bible says that there is a Friend who is much closer than a brother (Prov. 18:24). That Friend is Christ.

Early in the history of the earth, all of humankind joined together and erected a tower to try and reach heaven (Gen. 11). I believe in part that this was attempted due to a sincere need in the heart of humanity for God. To believe now, like the tower builders, that you have to get closer as a Christian in proximity to God is to be deceived in the same way Eve was in the Garden of Eden. She was tricked into believing that she needed to attain something that she already had. As a Christian, God is inside you. All you have to do is believe that He is in there.

When you feel something amazing, it doesn't mean that God just "showed up." In reality, it means that you are awakening to what's already there. You can feel His love because through intimacy with Him and meditation on Him, you awaken to the heavenly reality that He is in you and is all around you. His tangible love and powerful intimate presence are always there. He resides inside you. At times that feeling of His love and presence may seem to increase or decrease. However, the presence or absence of a feeling doesn't prove where God is or where God is not. The Bible proves where He is. It says that He doesn't ever leave you (see Deut. 31:6). Ever since the Holy Spirit came, you have been filled with 100 percent of His love and all the fruits of His Spirit. Through intimacy with Him, you are simply awakening to more and more. The more intimate time you spend with Him, the greater the reality that He is in you will be in your life.

ENCOUNTERING THE SUPERNATURAL

Now let's dive into the "supernatural encounter" portion of the secret place. It wasn't very long after God called me into the secret place that I began to have supernatural experiences with angels, God, and demons. I want to tell you about a few. Please remember from the Bible that God interacts with His people. Take a moment to reflect on the positive biblical encounters that you've read in scripture. Understand that Bible stories were never meant to simply make you smarter; they were meant for you to experience for yourself similar things and even greater things than you've read in the scriptures. Consider the verse in which Christ says, "I tell you the truth, anyone who believes in Me will do the same works I have done, and even greater works, because I am going to be with the Father" (John 14:12 NLT).

Jess and I had been married almost two years. I was a junior in college. Jess had a job at the local nursing home and had to leave the apartment very early in the morning. She woke me up to kiss me good-bye, and I walked down the hall to let her out and lock the door behind her as I had done many mornings. It was around five in the morning. I walked back to our bed feeling strange, really strange. Throughout the years, I've always been able to tell when something doesn't "feel" right. Even when I learned to avoid the conviction to "go home," I could always feel something was wrong. This morning it felt like there was a fight going on in my house. It's an awkward feeling when you see two people fighting in traffic, one yelling obscenities at the other. This is what this "felt" like. I had tightness in my chest, and there was such a tension in the room.

I had learned over the years about spiritual warfare and had prayed for people for healing—I had even by this point cast a few demons out of people. "Heal the sick, raise the dead, cleanse those who have leprosy, *drive out demons.* Freely you have received; freely give" (Matt. 10:8, emphasis mine). I knew what it felt like to be in a spiritual fight, and for whatever reason that morning one was going down in my bedroom. I began to pray. I prayed for good to triumph over evil. Still in prayer, I blinked, and standing over me at the foot of the bed was a six-winged angel. Two giant wings stretched out over the bed from the foot all the way to the head. Two wings covered the angel's face, and two wings were in back. I couldn't see his feet or lower body because of the footboard of the bed. This angel wasn't glowing like the angels on TV. His wings were solid white; in the dim room they were almost an off-white, with the natural morning light coming in through the blinds. The air was still and quiet as if time had stopped. Not a single sound bounced around that room. I couldn't breathe. I was in absolute shock—hyperventilating. There is no real way to describe this feeling. Sheer freaked-out terror.

Terrified, I blinked again, and he disappeared—or at least I couldn't see him anymore. I quickly grabbed a pen and paper, and drew a sketch of what he looked like so I wouldn't forget. I didn't know it at the time, but I would later learn that in the Bible are six-winged angels who fly around the throne of God. Check out the prophet Isaiah's encounter with them: "Above Him were the seraphim, each with six wings: With two wings they covered their faces, with two they covered their feet, and with two they were flying" (Isa. 6:2). I suppose that this angel was protecting me in that moment. At the time, I had read that angels were curious about the salvation that we get to take part in: "Even Angels long to look into these things..." (1 Pet. 1:12). So I did what I thought was appropriate. I began to preach right there in my room. I talked about why I love Jesus. I spoke of how much His love means to me and how it had changed me from the inside out. I figured that the angel might like to hear my heart. I believe he did.

That next day, I woke again and saw my wife off to work. I locked the door behind her, feeling an uneasiness again. I wondered if that angel might be back this morning. I lay back down in my bed and closed my eyes. Immediately, a warm feeling covered me. It felt like an overwhelming, incredible amount of tangible love. I saw a blue light in the room without opening my eyes. I could feel that on either side of the bed there was something standing there that was giving off a blue light. I remember that I felt like I began to move up and down through my feet. I remembered the Apostle Paul writing about out-of-body experiences—these must have been pretty tough to describe. Consider the verse: "I know a man in Christ who fourteen years ago was caught up to the third heaven. Whether it was in the body or out of the body I do not know—God knows" (2 Cor. 12:2). I wondered after this experience if this same thing that happened to Paul was about to happen to me. Slowly I was beginning to float off the bed! I immediately freaked out and was drawn back to the bed. Looking back, I remember this same exact thing happening a good bit as a child, and each time when I freaked out, it quit and I was drawn back.

These experiences only deepened my desire for the supernatural. I didn't totally understand it, but I loved the mystery and fun I was having with God. I felt my love for God increasing tremendously every single day. Every day was a new adventure.

That following night, I went to sleep, praying, "God, I've had angels visit me, I want You to visit me." I went to sleep so excited to wake up. I woke up and saw Jess off, kissing her good-bye. I shut the door, locked it, and walked hesitantly back to our bedroom. As soon as I got in bed and rolled over, I saw a light shoot out of the hallway. I thought to myself, *I know I didn't leave the light on.* I tried to roll over but couldn't. I couldn't move! The light came slowly to the side of my bed. I couldn't see where the light was coming from. It felt as if a million watts of power were surging behind me, and then it touched me. The love I could tangibly feel in my body was greater than I'd ever experienced in my life. I literally could feel warmth and love all over my paralyzed body.

Suddenly, the light was gone. I got up to check the hallway—no light was on. I knew that I hadn't left a light on! How was I to explain this stuff to my wife? Would she think I was crazy? Of the many stories I'd told her, this had to top them all. I talked with her on the phone later that day. I told her that something strange happened that morning. Immediately, she cut me off in the conversation. She said something strange had happened to her as well. She said that after I saw her off and locked the door, she got into her car like normal. She said, "As I pulled out of the driveway, I saw a black man walking toward our apartment dressed in an all-white pressed dress suit, white dress hat, and shined white dress shoes. He was wearing white from head to foot." We realized that the two stories were connected, and we went silent, stunned.

The next day I woke up early, ready for the supernatural. As I watched Jessica leave the house, I expected something would happen, and I was ready. I walked back to my bed and lay down. I heard in my heart, "If you want to see Me, sit up." I sat up quickly, but nothing happened. I heard, "If you want to see Me, get up and go into the hallway." So I did, and nothing happened. I heard, "If you want to see Me, go and put your nose an inch away from the front door's window." I walked over to the door, and as I leaned in, a sparrow flew from a nearby tree and landed less than an inch from my nose and looked at me for two seconds, eye to eye, before flying away. I was stunned. I praised God and laughed. I was in awe. What could I do? I had no words, as God was interacting with me. I knew that God loved me. The journey that the Lord had me on was making me realize that He wanted to be around me. He wanted my attention. He wanted my heart and my time. He was pulling me into intimacy—to a special place with Father and Son. "Now if we are children, then we are heirs—heirs of God and coheirs with Christ" (Rom. 8:17).

A few days later, Jess's car was in the shop, and I had to go pick her up. As I sat in my car waiting for her, I heard in my heart the word "Hello!" I hesitantly said, "Hello?" The voice said, "My name is Hello!" Oddly enough, immediately a song called "Hello Love" began to play on the radio. I laughed a little and just sat there. I heard the voice ask, "Do you believe I'm real?" I said nothing. To be honest, I'd began to wonder if I'd lost my mind. I heard, "Don't look toward the building your wife works in. Count down from ten, and she will be here." I began to count, still a little nervous about what I supposedly was hearing. As I counted, it was so hard for me not to look at the building. "...Five...four...three...two...

one." Literally, on number one, my wife grabbed the door handle, opened the door, and got in. I wasn't sure how to tell her what happened, but I did the best I could.

I could have easily written these experiences and others off as coincidence, maybe something I ate, maybe I was crazy. However, I had good mentors and a great friend who encouraged me to keep going and to stay within biblical bounds. I wasn't doing anything unbiblical. The Lord was communicating and interacting with me, as I was communicating and interacting with Him (James 4:8). If you're questioning these experiences in your heart, I want you to pause and reflect on things you've read from the Bible. All happenings that involve a supernatural God are different and, most of the time, a little strange.

In the month that followed, I began to hear God in the most intimate ways. I would go for walks and talk to the Lord about the simplest things—nothing that was serious. I made small talk with God about the rain, about my favorite car, about the little details of my day. While reflecting on this, I thought, *God wants to hear about my day even though He was there the whole time.* I noticed this when I was sitting down at the dinner table with my wife and my oldest child. I just wanted them to tell me how their day was. I didn't really care how unimportant they thought the minor details were. The important thing was that they talk to me and I respond in a loving way.

So I began to talk to the Lord about what I thought was the craziest stuff! I once remember having a conversation with God about my favorite animal at the zoo. I then proceeded to tell God about my favorite sport. I told God, "One thing I've never played a real game of is golf." I said, "It must be pretty hard because—" I was cut short by something shiny on the ground that caught my eye. I bent over, looked at it, and couldn't believe my eyes. I was speechless. I had never played a real round of golf, but I had played it in my backyard enough to know what I had just found. On the ground, right in from of me on the walking path, was a button marker from a golf glove.

It wasn't long before my prayer and worship life grew out of control. My love for God was through the roof. Everyone I met had to know of my love. Slowly, very slowly, God was lifting my love for Him over my work for Him. I was walking into the secret place of God.

EXPLAINING THE SUPERNATURAL

One thing that's always weighed heavily on my heart is the phrase "You can't explain some things; some things God doesn't want us to understand." I think that statement is true...sometimes. There are times when you don't need to understand something and should accept it by faith. However, there are truths of God in this book that I hope you can get a deeper grasp on—some things that we should understand, at least to a degree. One thing in particular is that you and God are able to interact. I hope you understand that the things I've written here are only the beginning for you. If God would be intimate with me, He truly would be intimate with anyone. By opening your heart, you will go far beyond any of my supernatural experiences in your own journey with the Lord. I really am excited for you!

In interacting with Him, please don't push Him away by trying to *understand* everything. The more time I spend with Him, the more I realize that He truly is unfathomable, unthinkable, and overwhelmingly uncomprehendable. All I ever want to do anymore is make sure I'm following a biblical way of thinking and run with Him. Trying to completely—or partially—understand Him is vastly unachievable. I think He likes it that way. There comes a moment in every marriage when we lose some of the mystery we had when we were dating. The days become routine, we can predict our spouse's every move, and so we have to work on our marriages. We have to cultivate the passion and mystery we had in the beginning and help it grow intentionally. Our relationship with God, however, will never lose its wonder, its mystery, or its passion. How could it? He is endless. The funny thing to me is that He looks at us with the same wild-eyed wonder as we look at Him. What kind of mystery would there be if we could fully understand all His ways?

FACE-TO-FACE PRAYER MODEL

The presence of God and supernatural encounters are going to appear throughout your journey with God. However, I encourage you to specifically ask God for them, just as Moses asked: "Now show me Your glory" (Exod. 33:18). As a blood-bought, born-again believer, think of how much more access to God you have than even Moses in the Old Covenant. I encourage you to be brave and ask amazing, powerful questions.

Step 1

Find a quiet spot that is free of distractions.

Step 2

Turn on some worship music that is God-focused and positive, just like we discussed. (See Phil. 4:8)

Step 3

For starters, spend ten minutes letting your mind run with thoughts of God. I encourage you to meditate on the song that is playing. Begin to let God draw on your chalkboard like we discussed earlier in chapter 6.

Step 4

Now intentionally ask God for encounters just like Moses did. I encourage you in this. You can ask for much more than Moses ever could. You are in Elyon. Ask God to open your eyes and open your heart.

The first time doing this should take about twenty minutes, so again set up a worship playlist that is around twenty-five minutes long.

Have fun, and enjoy your time. Don't get too serious. God is fun. He is always joking with me and having fun because He is my friend. I encourage you to joke around with Him as well. He wants to be your best Friend and Dad, not your impersonal distant "Higher Power" or distant and uninterested "Big Guy in the sky." He wants to come as close intimately as He is in proximity. It's up to you to engage Him with intimacy first.

8

Into the Secret Place, Part 4: Marriage with Christ

As the scripture says, "For this reason a man will leave his father and mother and unite with his wife, and the two will become one." There is a deep secret truth revealed in this scripture, which I understand as applying to Christ and the Church.

—Ephesians 5:31–32 GNB

I want you to read the first portion of this chapter, contemplating on the love my wife and I shared on the day we married. Jesus's heart for you is the same as my heart for my wife. We, being the Church, are the Bride of Christ. I want you to study my heart for her and notice the profound symbolism of Christ and His Church—Christ and His Bride.

OUR WEDDING STORY

It was May 11, 2007. My campus pastor and some of my best buddies had thrown me a bachelor's party before the big wedding day. We played cards, laughed, and joked around. I will never forget the joy on everyone's faces as we celebrated my big day, which was to come the following morning.

It was hard for me to go to sleep that night. I lay awake staring at the ceiling for hours, daydreaming about my soon-to-be wife and the life we would have together. I thought of our future. I wondered what our kids would look like. I hoped one would look like me. I wanted to be with her that night—but I had to wait. Despite my excitement, I wanted to make sure I was in His will. I prayed, "Lord, if this is not Your will, let me know," and then rolled over to try to get some sleep.

Just as I was drifting off, I heard God say in an audible voice, as if you and I were talking together, "I have brought you into the land I have given you." My eyes flew open, and a little tear of joy meandered slowly down the side of my face and onto the pillow. I knew for certain—Jessica was my promise.

I remember the wonderful day we were married like it was yesterday. I woke up early in the morning and went to my parents' house, where my dad helped me get my tux on and get ready for the wedding. I could see tears of love behind my dad's warm eyes as he helped me with my tie. The air was full of a quiet feeling that a beautiful season was ending, while a new, equally beautiful one was beginning.

We arrived at the church, and everyone was hurrying to get things done. The groomsmen rushed me to the nursery in the back room of our little brick country church, where I waited. I saw the old leather Bible I had always brought with me on the pulpit being stored there, and I sat down in the creaking brown rocker in front of the window. I fantasized to myself where Jess was and what she must look like. I imagined her with her friends around her, helping her get ready. I thought of what she must look like with someone fixing her hair. I thought of how beautiful she must be in the white dress that she had done a spectacular job of hiding from me for the past six months. Anxious thoughts filled my heart. I was ready to see her! I was nervous but so ready.

After ten minutes, our wedding planner came to my little room and told me that it was time for mine and Jessica's "moment." I was to see her for a few minutes before we took pictures. Excited and nervous, I jumped to my feet, adjusted my tie, and fixed my hair. Palms sweating, I took a deep breath and followed the wedding planner down the little hallway that led to the sanctuary. I quickly reminisced about the many times over the years that I had walked down that hall. I thought of my baptism. I thought of my old pastor calling me a turkey, as a friend and I gobbled up the leftover communion. I thought of Sunday school, where Jess and I had so much fun teaching. I thought of how cute Jess looked teaching all the children the vacation Bible school dances. I thought of the many late nights I had driven to the church alone and cried at the altar for her hand. I had prayed for this day, and finally it had arrived.

I was led across the sanctuary floor and then was told to face the pulpit with my eyes closed and not to turn around until I was told to do so. Heart pounding, I waited and waited. I then heard her laugh as the front door of the church opened—so joyful, so beautiful that my heart jumped as I smiled uncontrollably. I heard the sound of her dress as she moved closer and closer. *Swoosh, swoosh, swoosh.* I could hear every move she made, my heart beating faster and faster, my heart singing louder and louder. It felt as if my heart was reaching with all its strength toward her. Suddenly, the sound of her dress stopped, and I felt time was suspended. My heart was beating *bump, bump, bump,* and I could hear it beating in my throat.

Suddenly, I heard someone say, "You can look now!" I turned, and there she was. My bride! My love! My own! Tailor-fitted by God—for me! She was the definition of beauty. She had the biggest smile on her face. We were so excited that we quickly jumped into each other's arms. I could see in her eyes her love for me—and I could feel in my heart my love for her. I wanted to kiss her so bad, but she wanted to wait until we said "I do." We whispered sweet things to each other and laughed. "I can't wait until we get out of here!" I whispered as we both giggled. "I do...OK, let's go!" I said, and we laughed. We both blushed a little as we whispered sweet little things to each other—joyfully celebrating the moments we would share later that night. We hardly noticed the pictures being taken of us as we held each other's nervous hands.

As we looked into each other's eyes, I could see forever. I could see our children being born. I could see our first house. I could see us growing old together. Outshining everything else, I saw something more precious than anything I could ever want in her big brown eyes. I saw for the first time a love more precious than anything I could have ever hoped for. I saw a love, a true love—for me. Under tears and diamonds, I saw the love of my life! I saw Jessica! I saw my bride!

Too soon, our pre-wedding moment was over. The wedding planner could barely pull us away from each other. We proceeded to take pictures now with our entire wedding party. Laughter filled the sanctuary as we posed this way and that way. Before I knew it, I was rushed off to the little nursery again to await my "time."

The church filled with excitement and anticipation along with a roar of chatter and laughing. People began showing up by the masses, and before long the place was packed—people I knew, people I thought I knew, and others I was sure I had never met in my life.

Although I had heard from the Lord that Jess was my promise over a dozen times, including the night before, I asked Him again, hesitantly, under my breath, "Is this Your will?" I slowly opened the Bible I had left on the extra pulpit. The pages opened directly to a scripture that read, "I will make a new covenant with the house of Israel and the house of Judah" (Jer. 31:31 ESV). Today I was to make a new covenant with my fiancée and with God. My heart filled with such excitement and joy, I could barely stand it! God confirmed His word once again in my anxious heart. It was then that I heard one of my groomsmen say in a hushed voice, "Woody, it's time!"

MARRIED BY FAITH

"As the scripture says, 'For this reason a man will leave his father and mother and unite with his wife, and the two will become one.' There is a deep secret truth revealed in this scripture, which I understand as applying to Christ and the Church" (Eph. 5:31–32 GNB). The Bible is full of wild people who did extreme things with their faith. I would love it if you would take a moment and read Hebrews 11, known as the "hall of faith," in your favorite Bible before continuing any further. For your convenience, you can read it in the appendix at the end of this book.

Everything we do in life is done by faith. When you turn the faucet on in the shower, you have faith that the water will become hot...unless, of course, your hot water heater goes out like ours did recently. In that case, your stinky self will have to endure arctic-like temperatures from the faucet. When penguins show up to take a shower with you, you know you need a plumber. What a cold week that was for us! Likewise, when you turn the key in your car, you have faith that your car will start. When you get aboard an airplane, you have faith that it will lift itself off the ground and fly you safely thousands of miles through the air. When you sit down in a chair, you have faith that the chair will hopefully hold you.

In the same way, when we pray for salvation, we choose to believe by faith in what Christ has already done for us two thousand years ago. We believe by faith that His acts are enough to cover our sin. In the same way, when we pray with someone for healing, we believe by faith they will be healed. When Noah built the ark, he, by faith, expected a global flood, having never seen rain before. At that time, an early morning mist would come out of the ground and water the earth instead of rain like we have today (Gen. 2:6 NASB). Enoch and Elijah were both taken from the earth to heaven without ever dying—all by faith (Gen. 5:24 and 2 Kings 2:11). As we just read in Hebrews 11, it even says the earth was formed by faith. The same faith that formed the earth, also turns the faucet, accompanies you as you get on the plane, and heals the sick. It is also the very same faith that brings us in union with Christ. Galatians 3:26 GNB says, "It is through faith that all of you are God's children in union with Christ Jesus."

HANG IN THERE, FELLAS

You are called to an intimate union and marriage with Christ. If you are a guy and you have a problem with being a "Bride," then I want you to realize that He isn't calling you to become a woman or have those traits. He is not stripping you of your manhood. "Husbandry" is actually loving, nurturing, and protecting. We can see some attributes of the word husbandry as it is used in agriculture to refer to growing, protecting, and nurturing livestock. Let's read Psalm 23. Notice how the Shepherd husbands us:

The Lord is my shepherd, I lack nothing.
He makes me lie down in green pastures, He leads me beside quiet waters, He refreshes my soul.
He guides me along the right paths for His name's sake.
Even though I walk through the darkest valley, I will fear no evil, for You are with me; Your rod and Your staff, they comfort me.
You prepare a table before me in the presence of my enemies.
You anoint my head with oil; my cup overflows.
Surely Your goodness and love will follow me all the days of my life, and I will dwell in the house of the Lord forever.

The use of the word *husbandry* in shepherding livestock can help us see our relationship with Christ more clearly. However, we should continue to remember that the relationship is that of a marriage. It is quality time, gifts, affirmation, physical touch, acts of service, encouragement, protection, and intimacy. It's a marriage. You are infinitely more precious than cattle. You were created in His image as a partner—a relational match for Him to love and cherish. He cherishes you so much, He actually knows how many hairs are on your head (Luke 12:7).

SHADOWS
Anytime an artist creates something, you can see a little of his or her character in the work. This is considered the artist's "shadow." God is the ultimate artist. You can see Him in His work all around you. Everywhere are shadows and metaphors of who He is, because He is the artist. I want to briefly help you unpack how sex in marriage is a metaphor and a shadow of Christ and His Church—not that Christ in any way has sex with His Church, but it is a shadow of what happens between them.

Consider this: a child is conceived as a result of sexual intimacy between a husband and wife. This union has God's signature, just like everything He creates. When a man and woman unite in their hearts and their bodies in sex, the highest degree of human intimacy, a child is produced. Literally, life itself is created. A bride's reproductive organs were created by God to receive and grow life received from her husband. As a shadow, in intimacy with God (the highest attainable degree of intimacy), life is also created within you. That life grows, is nurtured, and is birthed into the rest of the world, just like a baby.

THE "POSITION" OF "THE BRIDE"

As the Bride, it is important for a Christian to realize that in the aspect of *position* you are already united with Christ. "Therefore, if anyone is in union with Christ, he is a new being! His old life has passed away; a new life has begun!" (2 Cor. 5:17 TCNT). What is often left undone in our experience is the second half of this verse: to *believe* that you are a new creation. Oftentimes we hear the concept that our past is gone, but this concept remains as knowledge in our minds and not a reality we experience. In 2 Corinthians 5:17, you are not only presented with the fact of your position of Bridal unity with Christ, but also presented with a solution to your unbelief in that fact. The solution is that when you come into unity (in the aspect of a deep intimacy in your heart) with Christ, you will realize that your past is really gone. You will also realize that you are a new creation and that everything really has become new about you. Every spiritual struggle dies as you remain the Bride in your heart. This verse also moves from a fact you simply have memorized to a reality you experience. All problems and issues you're dealing with, from your past and present, leave from your mind as His love and our love for Him outshines them.

Hebrews 12:2 speaks of "fixing our eyes on Jesus." In this niche of the secret place, the mind is totally fixed on a Bridal love with Him. In Godly meditation, it can be a temptation to try and figure out what God may be showing us. However, in this state of Bridal love, we have moved past that. Christ totally becomes our fixation. Our eyes are completely on Him. All the different stuff you may have experienced in the past fades in comparison to just being with Him. Nothing else matters except adoring and enjoying His presence and all He is. Lots of neat stuff can happen, but as I mentioned, concern for it literally vanishes as it's all overshadowed by love for Christ.

As the old song says, "Turn your eyes upon Jesus; look full in His wonderful face and the things of earth will grow strangely dim in the light of His glory and grace." Many times I have been in this aspect of the secret place and tried to think of problems I have or some sort of issue I may be dealing with, and I simply can't recall any of it. When your heart is in Bridal union with Him, the fact that "Jesus is all you need" becomes real. You are swallowed up in infinitely growing love and intimacy of marriage with Jesus, your Husband.

MARRIAGE WITH CHRIST PRAYER MODEL
Here we will combine what we learned in the previous chapters with what we learned in this one. Doing so will take you a little further in your journey with God. Let's dive in.

Step 1
Find a quiet spot that is free of distractions.

Step 2
Turn on some worship music that is God-focused.

Step 3
For starters, let your mind run with thoughts of God. Try to center your focus on God Himself, not the visions and revelations. Don't focus on a vision or thought to the point that you are distracted from God Himself. The intimacy with God you will experience is more important than a vision or revelation, although it is likely that you will remember the experience and revelation obtained from it. The most important revelation you can ever receive is of His intimate love for you. Simply focus on God and intimacy with Him.

Step 4
Intentionally begin to focus on Christ as a husband. You really have to be intentional here. This is a place to really press in and focus. If you

have a negative view of a husband, this may be difficult in the beginning. However, as you devote more and more time to this type of prayer, thoughts of love will swell in your mind as your heart overflows with love for Him. As you are awakened to the reality of His presence, you may experience many supernatural things—be brave and be biblical.

Before we move on, I want to encourage the men again. The manliest thing you can do is fall deeply in love with Jesus. This love, as I mentioned, has absolutely nothing to do with sex. This is a supernatural love that transcends everything you think you know about love and intimacy. The bravest thing you can do in the face of a Godless and chaotic society is to choose to love God extravagantly. Choose to be intimate with Him. It's the greatest and most daring adventure you will ever experience.

I will share with you at the beginning of the next chapter a personal story of what intimacy with God can do in someone's life. It is a story of a very dear friend of mine whom I led to the Lord simply by leading him to intimacy with God. He asked me for help, and I pointed him to Jesus. There wasn't a long, confusing trail of do's and don'ts. His life will never be the same.

When you travel the way that seems most pleasurable to you, it's much like starting a fire in your fireplace. Once the smoke begins to be drawn up the chimney, it will naturally continue to go up the chimney as long as there is a fire. Once you realize how easy and free it is to fulfill yourself through your marriage with Christ, instead of something lesser, it will become more difficult for you to stop fulfilling yourself with Him than it will be to sin.

9

Into the Secret Place, Part 5: The Fountain of Life

The previous chapter on marriage with Christ should be the focus of your life. In this chapter, you will learn about the wonderful byproducts of that marriage. In John 4, Jesus talks with a woman at a well. He tells her that if she were to drink from the water He had to offer, then she would never thirst again. Jesus is the well of living water, the fountain of life. As a result of intimacy with the fountain of life, you will never thirst again. Gatorade can't hold a candle to living water! Let me tell you a story of a man who was metaphorically drinking Gatorade but traded up for living water.

JOHN'S STORY

I will never forget that night. I was sitting at the dinner table. It was the day after Thanksgiving, and my dad, my wife, and I were drinking coffee and talking about life when my cell phone rang. It was John! John and I go way back. Years earlier, I'd had the privilege of leading John to Christ. Over time, I had become a mentor to him. Due to a house move, John and I had lost touch. I was excited to hear from him!

John sounded like he was in trouble, so I asked him what was going on. John told me that he had started smoking dope again. He had been in and out of rehab when the urge for the drug once again overtook him. He started smoking forty dollars' worth of the stuff a day. As a result of the drugs, he said that he had slapped his wife and had been kicked out of the house. He had been living at his job for the past few months. His wife now wanted a divorce.

John wanted to get better, but it seemed as though there was nothing he could do to escape his addiction. He mentioned that he had talked to a pastor who had invited him to a prayer meeting. He also mentioned he was going to try to start trying to read his Bible more and "learn" to be a "good Christian." Although I knew all this would help, I also knew that this man needed something much more—he needed intimacy with his Creator.

As I listened to his broken story, in a desperate voice he said, "Woody, anything I got to do to get my wife and kid back, I'll do."

I paused for a moment and stepped away from the table. As I walked to my bedroom, I could feel the tension and urgency of the moment. My response surprised Him. I said, "You want to really get high?" That night I led John to intimacy with the Lord. As a byproduct of the intimacy he found, he got "high," and he has never gone back to the counterfeit high of dope. He has found a greater high than the one he paid forty dollars a day for, completely free.

> Come everyone who thirsts, come to the waters; and he who has no money, come, buy and eat! Come, buy wine and milk without money and without price. Why do you spend your money for that which is not bread, and your labor for that which does not satisfy? Listen diligently to Me, and eat what is good, and delight yourselves in rich food. (Isa. 55:1–2 ESV)

John called me a few weeks later, asking if I could help him pick out some Christian CDs. He was with his wife and daughter at a Christian bookstore buying CDs! I was so thankful that he was free! John had moved back into the house with his family. He had his family back because intimacy with Jesus is more pleasurable than dope.

John shared what intimacy with God was doing for him at Narcotics Anonymous meetings, where he led other addicts to freedom through intimacy with God. He shared with me that a fifty-two-year-old lady, who was in one of his meetings, encouraged him privately, "You don't know it, but you're my inspiration."

THE MOUNTAIN OF PLEASURE

I want you to picture John on the side of a mountain. He thinks he is as high as he can climb. He believes he is at the top of the mountain, and then John chooses to look up. He sees that there is a higher place he can go. So he climbs to the highest point he can find, the highest point on the mountain. That point is Jesus Christ. That mountain is the mountain of pleasure. Christ, he realizes, is at the top. John sees that Christ could offer him a greater pleasure than that of dope.

The answer to overcoming your problem isn't to overcome evil with evil, or to overcome evil with restriction and self-discipline, but to overcome evil with good (see Rom. 12:21). Christ Himself said that the only "good" one is God. "'Why do you call Me good?' Jesus answered. 'No one is good—except God alone.'" (Luke 18:19). Therefore, we must not overcome evil with evil but overcome evil with God. The problem isn't that John or his friends wanted to get high. The problem was that they were silently told by the church culture that they couldn't find pleasure in Jesus—so they turned to dope. He was left with no real option. It's sad to think about, but how many times have we demonized people for wanting to fill a void within themselves?

DESIRE OF THE NATIONS

Every desire you have in your life can be fully satisfied in Christ. "Take delight in the Lord, and He will give you the desires of your heart" (Prov. 37:4). Literally, by taking delight in the Lord in intimacy (which is your purpose), you will find that your calling and destiny are plopped right into your lap naturally, without striving for them.

The Bible says that Christ is the desire of the nations. Remember the verse in which Haggai prophesied referring to Christ in this way: "And I will shake all nations, and the desire of all nations shall come: and I will fill this house with glory, saith the Lord of hosts" (Hag. 2:7 KJV). Through intimacy with Him, I believe that we as Christians will begin to reveal to the nations what and who it is that they actually desire. It's not oil, it's not power, it's not land—it is, however, intimacy with their Creator. Sadly, if we live our lives as though Christ is not our desire nor the desire of the nations, then He will seem as though He is not what He truly is. It is up to us, by falling in love with Christ and enjoying intimacy with Him ourselves, to show every nation all over the world that He is what they desire.

CREATED FOR PLEASURE

Humans were created in the Garden of Eden. *Eden* translates as the Hebrew word "pleasure." The Garden was called pleasure for two reasons. The first reason was that pleasurable trees had been gathered to one spot as a home for the first man and the first woman (see Gen. 2:9). The second and primary reason the Garden's name was "pleasure" is because God dwelt with His people there. "In Your presence is fullness of joy; In your right hand there are pleasures forevermore" (Ps. 16:11). He was intimate with the first man and woman there. After the fall and humanity's removal from the garden, humans kept their inner makeup as citizens of pleasure. Think about this: when you take a fish out of water, it is still a fish. The fish is still designed to live and breathe in water, regardless of if it is in water or not. In this same way, when humans were removed from the garden, they still needed pleasure. Humans have continually searched for it in money, sex, drugs, and power since the fall, when the ultimate source of pleasure—intimacy with God—was taken away. Jesus died for all men and women as a spotless sacrifice and payment for the sin that threw humans from the garden and from intimacy with God. Through the blood of Jesus Christ, humans now have access to the source of all pleasure once again—an intimate relationship with God.

You, being a citizen of pleasure, will travel the way that seems most pleasurable to you. When you fulfill your need for pleasure with intimacy with God, you will realize that you do not need the lesser pleasures of pornography, drug addiction, money addiction, sex outside of marriage, or any other self-destructive behavior. You must point the desires in your heart for pleasure toward God and true fulfillment, or you will become enslaved in an attempt to fulfill yourself through addiction and sin.

Initially, with drugs, you have an amazing feeling of invincibility and satisfaction. Afterward, you are stuck forever trying to get back to that feeling of pleasure. In the secret place with God, you have an amazing experience, and each time, your experience with Him grows. Being with Him gets more and more pleasurable every day. As your faith increases with each moment with God, so too increases the amount of that reality you awaken to. It's not that somehow His presence increases—He is in you right now fully—but your awareness and consciousness of it increases. The Bible says we are constantly moving from the state that we are in to a greater state: "And we all, who with unveiled faces contemplate the Lord's glory, are being transformed into His image with ever-increasing glory, which comes from the Lord, Who is the Spirit" (2 Cor. 3:18).

The same intimacy that set John free of his drug addiction will iron out all other issues in life. There is a God-shaped keyhole in everyone's heart that only God can satisfy. He created you this way so that an intimate relationship with Him would be your only option for satisfaction and fulfillment. John learned that the desire in his heart for a high was actually a desire placed by God for intimacy with Him. That intimacy would take him higher than anything on the planet.

Just like John, you have needs and a desire for intimacy. You may not be addicted to drugs, but you may have issues and problems in your life that arise daily. Being aware of God's presence is the most satisfying, fulfilling, and freeing experience you could ever attain. All of your needs can be met daily in a one-stop shop—your Husband, Jesus.

ARE YOU BORED?

If your life since you became a Christian is boring and unfulfilling, chances are you haven't walked into real intimacy with God. God's heart is not that you be restricted from pleasure and excitement by principles found in the scriptures, but that you are directed toward the most powerful pleasure and excitement by the scriptures. His heart is that you realize that He is the fulfillment of all pleasure. "You make known to me the path of life; You will fill me with joy in Your presence, with eternal pleasures at Your right hand" (Ps. 16:11).

Sadly, Christians often live their lives in constant states of self-induced restrictions, believing that God is going to somehow numb them to their natural desires for pleasure. The truth is exactly the opposite. Your desire for pleasure will only grow as you realize that there is no limit to the amount to be had in Him. People with addictions, hurt, or bondage only need to be pointed toward the real source of all pleasure, and they will leave a lesser, counterfeit one behind.

THE FOUNTAIN OF LIFE PRAYER MODEL

Step 1
Find a quiet spot that is free of distractions.

Step 2
Turn on some worship music that is God-focused and positive, just like we discussed in prior chapters.

Step 3
For starters, let your mind run with thoughts of God. Try to center your focus on God Himself, not the visions and revelations. Don't focus on a vision or thought to the point that you are distracted from God Himself. The intimacy with God you will experience is more important than a vision or revelation, although it is likely you will remember the experience and revelation obtained from it. The most important revelation you can ever receive is of His intimate love for you. Simply focus on God and intimacy with Him.

Step 4

Intentionally begin to focus on Christ as a Husband. You really have to be intentional here. This is a place to really press in and focus. If you have a negative view of a husband, this may be difficult in the beginning. However, as you devote more and more time to this type of prayer, thoughts of love will swell in your mind as your heart overflows with love for Him.

Step 5

Let the feelings of love for Christ well up in you and satisfy you. I encourage you to open your heart and let Him express His tangible love for you as well. Remember, though, you must engage Him first and draw near to Him (James 4:8). Be biblical, and be free.

If you feel like you're having trouble moving forward in intimacy with Christ, get up and try doing something different. Dance or sing, "make music from your heart to the Lord" (Eph. 5:19). You will find yourself moving in deep intimacy with God before you know it.

DON'T GET DISCOURAGED

In the beginning, I beat myself up inside in moments when I felt I wasn't experiencing what I assumed I was supposed to experience. The reality is that you are married even when you don't "feel" like it. Your marriage is the focus and goes far beyond a feeling. While there are extreme feelings associated with intimacy with Christ, don't be condemning toward yourself if you don't always "feel" something. Just enjoy your marriage.

A PROPOSAL

I propose that you can live in the secret place. Normal life can happen as you are simultaneously, absolutely overwhelmed by Christ. The more you stay in an intimate place with God, the easier you will find yourself conscious of the deep levels of it. You are simply awakening to a consciousness of what already exists because of what Christ has done for you. My thoughts constantly race with God and Christ, no matter my situation.

I wake up, and my first thought is something about God. At work, I am constantly conscious of Him and communing with Him. Even if I'm joking around, God is still at the center of my mind. Christ is always my focus. These thoughts aren't the result of some forced habit; I am simply in love.

Overwhelming love and satisfaction over who God is will soon become your lifestyle—as thoughtless as choosing your favorite coffee cup. It changes who you naturally are. You naturally, without *effort*, will love God and love people, and in doing so you will walk right into your destiny. Consider the verse:

> And you, dear brothers and sisters, are children of the promise, just like Isaac. But you are now being persecuted by those who want you to keep the law, just as Ishmael, *the child born by human effort*, persecuted Isaac, *the child born by the power of the Spirit*. But what do the Scriptures say about that? "Get rid of the slave and her son, for the son of the slave woman will not share the inheritance with the free woman's son." So, dear brothers and sisters, we are not children of the slave woman; we are children of the free woman. (Gal. 4:28–31 NLT, emphasis mine)

You are not the son or daughter born out of human effort. Christ Himself gave the effort for what you have freely. You are the children of the free woman—a son or daughter born by the power of the Spirit. Don't strive; just enjoy. "Come, everyone who thirsts, come to the waters; and he who has no money, come, buy and eat! Come, buy wine and milk without money and without price. Why do you spend your money for that which is not bread, and your labor for that which does not satisfy? Listen diligently to Me, and eat what is good, and delight yourselves in rich food" (Isa. 55:1–2 ESV).

10

Into the Secret Place, Part 6: Overflow

Heidi Baker of Iris Ministries is one of my favorite people on this planet. She once said, "All fruitfulness flows from intimacy." She couldn't have been more right. In the dream I mentioned at the beginning of this book, I spoke of a bedroom that Christ entered. In the layout of the house, that bedroom was also a living room. You see, amazing person, you were meant to live in the bedroom of God. You were meant to live in intimacy in the secret place with Him. I want to take a moment here in the last component of the secret place to hopefully inspire you to live there. Everything you do for and with God is going to overflow from that place with Him.

As I spend time in the secret place, every single day becomes an adventure. Sometimes I feel like Indiana Jones in a spiritual way. This chapter is filled with adventure stories. To me, this is the most fun chapter of the whole book. It's a collection of some of my favorite stories of my adventures that stemmed from the overflow of the secret place. As you stay in that place with God, you too will have many adventures. Your love for God and for people will increase. You may just find yourself in a local crack house, leading a prostitute to Jesus. Who knows? Whatever the adventure, it will be fun, wild, and great. Please sit back, relax, and enjoy.

While I understand that these next stories may seem hard to believe, recall the stories you've read in the Bible. As long as it lines up with God's word, the word "strange" is normal to God and should be to every believer. In fact, God never did the same miracle the same way, ever.

REUNION WITH AN OLD FRIEND

When I was in second grade, I met and became best buds with a world changer, William Wood. We had a fight in the bathroom of Luverne Elementary School and have been best friends ever since. That was a horrible experience, and I really have no idea how we became friends after that, but we did. I remember that, around the third grade, William's house burned to the ground. My dad walked over and gave William a hug, as he was a forest ranger and was there to put the fire out. My mom encouraged me to help William by giving him a Bible, and so I did. In the fifth grade, I went to a different school, and as kids do, we parted ways. William and I went down separate paths and came back together in our early twenties. As it turned out, William had gotten saved and so had I. Mom encouraged me to call him. She even gave me his number. I, however, was reluctant to call, so my mom called him for me. She invited him over to my sister's apartment without me knowing it and then invited me over!

I remember talking to William from day one about Jesus. There is such a communion that he and I share that's hard to describe. We just enjoy God together. I know I was in God's will with William in the street ministry we both loved—although staying out past midnight with my wife at home wasn't in God's will, as I talked about in earlier chapters. Regardless, you could say that we were born into street ministry together. We met back up at the beginning of that season in both of our lives and began that journey out into the streets together. I can remember a day when Jess, William, and I went to the streets for over twelve hours. That day, we saw over one hundred people encouraged and healed of different diseases. During this period of my life, I was awakened to the power of God, the prophetic word, and the powerful meshing of the two. It would take a book by itself to write about all the miracles we saw during these years in the streets. Street ministry is today one of the most important aspects of my life and my family's life. Just yesterday, my daughter asked me to take her out on the streets again.

On the streets, I quickly became aware of the fact that, as the book of Job puts it, while God is speaking, we don't always perceive it: "For

God does speak—now one way, now another—though no one perceives it" (Job 33:14). I began looking for God's voice in *everything*. Receipts, pieces of trash on the highway, sunsets, and nature—everywhere I looked, I could find God's voice. Once we were riding in the car, and I started thinking about this verse. I asked, "Hey, William, what do you think that God is saying through that crow right there?"

William replied, "Direction to death."

I immediately whipped the car around and followed the bird. To anyone else, we would've looked crazy, but to William and me, it was the only logical thing to do. We saw the bird fly over a man's mobile home nearby. As we pulled down the dirt road to the house, I noticed that there was a very angry-looking man on the porch with a shotgun. Because of the gun and the look on this man's face, William and I thought, *Maybe this isn't direction to our death!* I pulled up near the trailer and rolled down the window. I asked, "Excuse me, sir, but we were led to this house to pray for someone. Is there anyone here who needs prayer?"

He said, "My son is inside dying of pneumonia."

We prayed for his son and believe God healed him. As we finished praying, we saw the bird again, and we followed it to another house. We stopped and a very sad lady came to the door. She looked to be in depression. We told her the story about the bird and asked if we could pray for her. She said, "Yes, my son and husband were just killed in a car wreck."

God lifted her heart from the pit. I believe she was encouraged by our prayers and love for her—again, "direction to death." When we finished praying, we saw the bird again. We followed it to her neighbor's house and got to pray for a pastor who was dying of cancer—again, "direction to death."

In case you are wondering, I do not follow crows today and haven't since that day. The words "direction to death" were the words for a moment. It was not meant to build a doctrine or belief around. Crows may never again mean "direction to death" in my life. This word, like everything, only works with the Holy Spirit's leading. The Lord is speaking in some way through everything around you. Are you listening for His voice?

One night, William and I felt led to go to Walgreens. When we got there, we had an urge to pray for someone—anyone—as there are always bunches of sick people at a Walgreens late at night. We saw a man with a sling on his arm in a blue hospital gown. He was walking slow and looked to be in pain. He'd come to the pharmacy to get pain medicine, but the pharmacy was closed. We asked him about his arm, and as it turned out, it was totally crushed. We prayed for the presence of God to fill the man's home, to dwell there and to heal him. As we had often done back then, we gave the man our phone numbers to let us know later how God moved in his life. The man called us about an hour later, screaming on the phone, "I can move my arm better than I ever have in my whole life!" He said, "When I entered my home I felt something, and now I am healed!"

These moments of seeing God's power began to shape the way I view sickness and disease. Sickness and disease are paid for by the blood of Jesus and are a trespass against what Christ has done. "He forgives all my sins and heals all my diseases" (Ps. 103:3 NLT). Be healed!

THE CAT STICKER
One night, Jess and I made a quick Wal-Mart run. On our rounds through the store, I saw a weird sticker of a smiling cat on the floor. It looked to have been there for a while, as it had clearly been buffed and waxed over with one of those giant machines. As we got in our car that night, the Lord said, "Go back and look at the cat sticker." Trusting Him, I went back into the store. As I entered the store, I bumped into an old buddy of mine who had torn his rotator cuff. His shoulder was in intense pain. I asked him if I could pray with him, and he said "Yes!" He was healed right there in Wal-Mart after we prayed twice.

AMAZING HAPPENINGS AT CHURCH
One Sunday, we got a chance to pray for an elderly lady whose legs were different lengths. One of her legs was two inches shorter than the other,

and this caused a ton of back pain for her. Weird as it was, as we were praying for about fifteen minutes, I witnessed her leg grow out a few inches to be even with the other one. She left church with legs of equal length and was absolutely pain-free.

On another Sunday, we prayed for a man's skin cancer that he had on the left side of his nose. As he was on his way home in his red pickup truck, only a mile from church, the cancer on his nose fell off in his lap. In addition to these miracles, we saw dozens of people healed at church of various diseases. However, the majority of the miracles we saw during this time were on the street.

B AND SAM

A couple of young men from Uzbekistan moved in next door ("B" and "Sam"). I really enjoyed these guys. One day, I decided to introduce myself. When I did, they invited me in their house. My heart broke. They had one chair and one table in their home: no other furniture, not even a bed. They offered me some hot tea, which I hesitantly drank. I found out they were in college. Being basically broke ourselves and also in college, we knew how hard that must be for them. Jess and I gave them tons of food—every bit of food we could spare. Eventually, our conversations over hot tea turned to Christ. It seems like they asked me every single hard question about Christianity imaginable. I almost always had an answer, and those questions I didn't have an answer for, I looked up for them.

"B" said one day, "You are the holiest person I know!" He even asked me if I was an angel, to which I laughed and told him no. "B" and "Sam" had been thinking of becoming Muslims. It seemed like Jess and I were in a constant struggle to see who could devote more time to these guys—us or the Muslims. I prayed that God would begin to reveal himself to "B" and "Sam" through dreams and signs. Jesus eventually appeared to "B" in a dream. In the dream was a man dressed in an off-white robe and hood. B asked Him, "Are you Jesus?" To which the man replied, "Yes, follow Woody." Through the relationships and love that God showed them through Jess and I, and through dreams and revelations, they believed in Christ over Islam.

MEDICAL SUPPLY

For almost a year, God opened a door in the way of a job at a medical supply store in town. I prayed for every person I visited and hoped they would get better. I wasn't sure if I was supposed to pray for people or not, so I never told my boss. One lady I prayed for was obese to the point that she couldn't stand or walk. I believe she weighed between four hundred and four hundred fifty pounds. She hadn't walked in seven years. Someone had to help her even go to the bathroom and get in her bed. I felt so sorry for her. She was one of the nicest ladies I'd ever met. While I set up her oxygen equipment, I can remember praying over her bariatric hospital bed and over her room. Before I left, I asked her softly if I could pray with her. She said, "Sure, honey," and I did. As it turned out, she loved the Lord very much.

A month went by and I assumed that she, like many others I had prayed for, didn't get her healing. But three months later that nice lady called my boss and told him that since the day I prayed for her, she had lost 130 pounds (in three months)! She said she was up walking down the hall! She could walk around her bed and do the dishes! She said she now weighed as much as she did when she got married. God answered her prayer and gave her mobility back! I was ecstatic! I loved the fact that she was healed because it helped her, not because I hated the demon causing her problems. Again, I could see my love for people continuing to grow as Jess and I stayed in the secret place.

"IF YOU HAVE A BABY, I WILL BLESS YOU"

Did you know that intimacy produces life? Of course you did. We discussed that in chapter 8. The closeness that Jess and I began to share led us to want a baby. It was ten o'clock at night. I was undressed. OK, I know this is too much information already, but hang with me. Jess and I had decided to conceive a child. We had already decided that we absolutely couldn't afford it, but God wanted us to trust Him. I had danced around the idea of a child for months. I had bought Jess a few fish, which all died. I was out of town when they died. Jess called me crying, and I tried to pray for resurrection over the phone for the fish, which didn't work. We had thrown around the idea of getting a puppy. I wondered how we could keep a human alive if we couldn't keep a few fish alive for two months. My wife didn't want a fish or a puppy—she wanted a baby. I will never forget hearing God's voice over and over: "If you have a baby, I will bless you." With dream after dream and confirmation after confirmation, we knew we could have a baby. So I had decided that I wanted a baby, too. I nervously stood in the kitchen, staring at my open Bible and searching the concordance for something about children to give me some courage. I found Psalm 127, which reads:

> Children are a heritage from the Lord, offspring a reward from him. Like arrows in the hands of a warrior are children born in one's youth. Blessed is the man whose quiver is full of them. They will not be put to shame when they contend with their opponents in court. (Ps. 127:3–5)

The second I read those few verses and had made up my mind that I had enough courage to go through with it—at ten o'clock at night I heard a knock at the door! I mean, I was standing at the bedroom door ready to go through with this! I thought, *Who in the world?* (Insert a few bad words in here as well.) I freaked out a little and pitched a silent but dramatic fit. I crept to the front door, still naked and a little ticked, and asked, "Who? Who is it?"

Of all people at ten o'clock at night, it was my mom! She said, "It's me, honey; is this a bad time?"

I said very quickly, "Yes, ma'am!"

She said, "OK, baby. Well, I just wanted to give you something. I'll just leave it on the doorstep."

I said, "OK, thank you! I love you."

She replied, "OK, baby, night-night," and walked back to my sister's apartment two doors down. At ten o'clock at night, naked and crouching behind the door, I reached my hand out and grabbed the little tissue my mom had left for me. I pulled it in through the door and slowly opened the tissue. I was in shock, because inside was a beautiful arrowhead. God confirmed once again His word to me! I had just read seconds ago before I opened the door, "Like *arrows* in the hands of a warrior are children born in one's youth" (Ps. 127:4, emphasis mine). I later awkwardly told my mom how she had encouraged me—she had no idea. My mom does this type of thing by accident constantly. I love getting around her and just letting her be herself. She encourages the heck out of me and seemingly never realizes it—it is just her nature.

God was teaching me to trust Him through this, by giving me a beautiful little girl. I began to notice that God interacts with us every single day in these shocking and dramatic ways. I believe He loves to surprise and awe us. However, like the verse I've quoted from the book of Job that says, "We don't always notice it," either we don't notice it or we write it off as coincidence. We must have a childlike faith in our approach to God to hear Him and not write it off as something else. "And He said: 'Truly I tell you, unless you change and become like little children, you will never enter the kingdom of heaven.'" (Matt. 18:3). "Truly I tell you, anyone who will not receive the kingdom of God like a little child will never enter it" (Luke 18:17). The closer I come into intimacy with God, the more I notice His voice all around me. In turn, the more I notice His voice, the deeper in intimacy I go with the Lord.

BUSYNESS AND DEPRESSION

When my oldest daughter was around three years old, I got too busy for intimacy with God. I walked into a spiritual depression that I couldn't explain and was desperately trying to shake. Literally, the life was sucked out of me by ministry. I never worshiped, prayed, or fasted anymore like I used to. In every spare moment, I chose to prepare for a sermon and never studied to learn. The most I read my Bible outside of sermon prep was at night with my daughter. I believe God used her in a major way to draw me back to the intimate secret place with Him.

Late one night, in the lowest place I'd felt in a long time, I asked Madelyn, my oldest, to anoint and pray for me. She had never heard of or seen anyone prayed over with oil. I ran and got some anointing oil and gave her the open bottle. She then, with no instruction from me, slowly poured oil on my head and face until it ran down on my beard. She then poured oil on my hands and carefully put it on each finger—front and back. She then said, "I want to pour it on your feet." I pulled off my shoes and socks, and she told me to sit on the floor. I watched as my three-year-old poured the remaining oil in the little jar on both of my feet and carefully on each toe and toenail. She looked up—I was weeping by this point—and said, "We're going somewhere!"

I said, "Where?"

She said, "On a boat ride."

In this moment, with oil running down my face, hands and feet, the Lord brought to mind these scriptures:

Peter, suddenly bold, said, "Master, if it's really You, call me to come to You on the water." He said, "Come ahead." Jumping out of the boat, Peter walked on the water to Jesus..." (Matt. 14:28–30 MSG)

Then the disciple whom Jesus loved said to Peter, "It is the Lord!" As soon as Simon Peter heard him say, "It is the Lord," he wrapped his outer garment around him (for he had taken it off) and jumped into the water." (John 21:7)

Notice that in both of these instances Peter actually got out of the boat to get to Jesus. He couldn't wait for the boat to get to shore! The Lord revealed to me in that moment that in both scriptures Peter leaped out of the boat because of his love for Jesus. In the first scripture in Matthew 14:28–30, Peter's overwhelming love for Jesus produced the faith he needed for walking on water. It was his love for Christ that created a platform he walked on to get from where he was to where he needed to be—the arms of Jesus. He wasn't worried if the water would hold him; that wasn't his focus. He leaped out of the boat to get to Christ, and his love for Him produced the miracle. Certainly God was drawing me to His love through this anointing with my little girl.

I am back to intimacy with the Father, knowing my love with Christ is going to change the world—naturally. My focus is Him. When given the choice of one or the other, loving on Jesus is more important than preparing to talk about Him. Loving Jesus naturally brings the faith that makes what you hope to achieve possible. Don't get me wrong, I do prepare for sermons, but that's not my focus. My focus is my love for Christ Himself. In all that we do, our focus should be intimacy and love with Christ.

TRUSTING HIM IN OUR FINANCES

To preface this paragraph, let me backtrack a little. When we got married, we couldn't afford it. We actually had seventy-five dollars when we got back from our honeymoon. Yes, that was all the money to our name... seventy-five dollars. When we decided to have our first child, I was to graduate college and be a new father in the same month. I sent my resume to thirty different businesses trying to get a job. Two offered to sell me, a recent (broke) college graduate, their business for two hundred fifty thousand dollars! When we decided to have our second child, Jess felt led to come home from working and raise a family. Our budget actually showed that we would be negative two hundred dollars a month with our current income. The Lord spoke to me, "Isn't your child worth two hundred dollars?" Again, we couldn't afford it, but we went for it, feeling God's leading.

Then God said we could move and buy a home of our own. Again, we couldn't afford it, but we went for it, based on God's leading. Then God said we could have a third child. Again we trusted, and he has provided. Even though in each and every one of these situations we never had the money initially, God always provided. God has taught me to trust Him despite our finances, to trust His voice and not logic. His word trumps every circumstance. Following His lead is key, I have learned, to walking in intimacy with Him.

LOVING THE POOR

God's passionate call isn't so often in what looks like the "safest" of places but in the most dangerous—where all you have to depend on is Him. He will provide. The "safest" place, after all, is in the center of His intimate will. I recently felt a strong urge to go do some street ministry at lunch because I just wanted to love the poor. So I prayed about it and decided that God wanted me to go down a nearby street. It just so happened that this street was one of the most dangerous streets in Montgomery, Alabama. Walking down the street, I saw broken-down houses, graffiti, and huge dogs. I got to the end of the street and decided to turn around. I couldn't find the people I felt led to pray for! On my way back, I heard some people cussing one another out. Naturally, I interrupted with a loud, "Hey! Can I pray for you guys?"

One lady said, "No, but there are some women across the street who might need some prayer."

I walked across the street to find a homeless shelter. I had unknowingly worked less than a mile from a homeless shelter for almost three years. For me, this was a gold mine. I went in and asked the management if I could pray for anyone. The man told me, "Sure, there's tons of people here." I walked to the back with him and entered a room full of people. He interrupted all of them and said, "Hey! This is Woody Money. He is a pastor from Troy. He is here to pray with you." Everybody got quiet and stared at me.

We just sort of looked at one another for a second as I awkwardly asked the nearest lady to me if she needed prayer for anything. She said no. I asked her if I could pray that God would bless her, and she gave a hesitant yes. When I started to pray, everyone in the room left except for me, her, and one other lady and her baby. It sounded like a huge herd of wildebeest just saw a lion...and were definitely not getting eaten for lunch. I guess I freaked them all out. While praying for this lady, I could barely hold my tears back. I wanted to be cheerful and bring these people joy, but I became so overwhelmed with love for them that I found it hard to keep it together. My heart felt like it was gushing with love for these people. As we prayed, I felt like the Lord wanted her to know that He was about to give her a truck, so I told her.

Before I prayed for the next lady, I asked her if I could talk to her for a second. She said yes. I asked her if she had any pain in her body. I will never forget the look of pain and hurt on her face as she hesitantly thought about that question. She said, holding her heart, "I'm hurt," as she began to cry.

I asked her, "Why are you hurt? What happened?"

She said, "My mom hurt me, and I can't forgive her."

This lady broke down in front of me. I asked her if I could pray with her for her to forgive her mom. As we prayed, I, in turn, broke down all over this poor woman in this homeless shelter. We were both crying. I realized that God had seen her pain and wanted to help her, so He sent me. He sent me into a homeless shelter in the hood to heal unforgiveness in the heart of a woman in her midthirties who had absolutely nobody and nothing. Even now it breaks my heart. God wanted to help her, even though to many people she was a seemingly "insignificant" and poor lady. Yet He sent me. I've been back to that shelter several times, and every time something incredible happens. On one of my most recent visits, I got a chance to share with a prostitute her identity in Christ. It was incredible to watch as her mind changed from what she thought of herself to what God thought of her.

DEEPER LOVE
Intimacy with God has given me a deeper love for my wife, my family, my Bible, and the people in the world around me. My wife and I now have a date night once a week. I love Jessica more today than ever. It's as if the more I awaken to a deeper love for Jesus, I automatically love my wife and others deeper as well out of the overflow. God has brought a beautiful

balance to my marriage. I still pray for people in and outside of Troy with my family and my church family. I make sure that I am following the voice of the Spirit in whatever I do, and I make sure to stay in the secret place. As a byproduct of the intimacy with God we now share, I am spiritually healthier than I've ever been in my life.

TREASURE HUNT

Every time Madelyn and I ride by Krystal's Restaurant in town, she says, "Look, Daddy, there's the treasure hunt place! When are we going back to the treasure hunt place?" "Treasure hunting" is simply asking God what He's doing in the city and joining Him. The "treasure" is those people God wants to touch. Recently, we prayed for fifty-two people in the street in four days. My daughter loves doing this. Oftentimes we find ourselves at different places in the city, praying with and encouraging people. I love my daughter and serving the Lord with her. I can't wait to do the same with my youngest daughter Ava and my son Josiah.

OVERFLOW PRAYER MODEL

Let's go on a treasure hunt. We are going to ask God what He is doing right now in your city and join Him.

Step 1
Find a quiet spot that is free of distractions.

Step 2
Turn on some worship music that is God-focused and positive as discussed in prior chapters.

Step 3
For starters, let your mind run with thoughts of God. Try to center your focus on God Himself, not the visions and revelations. Don't focus on a vision or thought to the point that you are distracted from God Himself.

The intimacy with God you will experience is more important than a vision or revelation, although it is likely you will remember the experience and revelation obtained from it. The most important revelation you can ever receive is of His intimate love for you. Simply focus on God and intimacy with Him.

Step 4

Intentionally begin to focus on Christ as a Husband. You really have to be intentional here. This is a place to really press in and focus. If you have a negative view of a husband, this may be difficult in the beginning. However, as you devote more and more time to this type of prayer, thoughts of love will swell in your mind as your heart overflows with love for Him.

Step 5

Let the feelings of love for Christ well up in you and satisfy you. I encourage you to open your heart and let Him express His tangible love for you as well. Remember, though, you must engage Him first and draw near to Him (James 4:8). Be biblical, and be free.

Step 6

Ask God what He is doing in the city and write it down. Use the template below to help you find your first treasure. Remember, the treasure is simply people God wants to impact. Finding the treasure requires that you listen to God's instruction and detail. I encourage you to ask these questions and write down God's answers without really thinking too hard.

- *God, who do You want to bless today?*
- *God, are they wearing anything special?*
- *God, where can I find them?*
- *God, what do You want to do with them?*
- *God, what is a word from Your heart for them?*

Step 7

Go find your treasure! Here's a hint: first, be brave, and second, be grace-ful. If God reveals some sort of sin that your "treasure" is involved in, sim-ply pray the solution. Do not call out sin. Always be positive, and have fun.

I would love to hear from you about your treasure hunt. My website is in the back of this book. Up next, we discuss the final topic of the secret place. We are coming in for a landing.

11

Final Word

Throughout this book, I have been very careful not to dishonor any part of the Church. By "the Church," I am speaking of fellowship with believers all over the world. I love "the Church." Any believer who hates or distances themselves from "the Church" because they believe differently than someone else will find themselves in error. You must embrace one another in your uniqueness, even if a part of your church, "the Church" or "the Body of Christ," isn't as "deep" in spiritual matters as you think you are. Humble yourself and love people. Do not talk badly of them for their beliefs. Love them. They are, in fact, a part of the Bride Jesus died for, and they are your spiritual brothers and sisters.

In your journey, I encourage you with this: if you find opposition to your feelings toward Christ or your views from fellow Christians, please do not run to leave the Church. Consider their beliefs and read your Bible; study to find the correct answers. You might be in the wrong, or God may use you as the change or light to them.

By "leaving the Church," I mean "to leave every church"—to break fellowship with the Body of Christ. I have seen many people I know leave the Church over their beliefs. You ask them, "What church do you go to?" They reply, "I don't do church." When you believe that the Church has nothing to offer you, you have been deceived and have likely been hurt. Church is a place where we should find constant fellowship and healing. It is a community. Consider carefully leaving or switching communities. Even in the television show *The Lone Ranger*, the Lone Ranger wasn't really alone—he had Tonto! You were created to run with a pack. When you become a truly "Lone Ranger," you will begin to walk in deception. There is only one reason you should leave the specific church you attend. That one reason is "God's leading." If He does lead you to move churches, do so with honor and do not remain out of fellowship. Go to church where He leads you.

WHY I HATE THE LIBRARY

I hate the library. Not because I hate to read; I actually love to read. I love history, and I love books! The reason I hate the library is the same reason many people hate going to church. The sad reality is that in many churches what oftentimes is offered is tons of information—like a library—but little to no celebration. The world doesn't need a library full of "Shush—be quiet!" The world needs a Bride celebrating her Husband!

WHY I HATE THE DOCTOR'S OFFICE

The reason I hate the doctor's office is similar. It has nothing to do with fear of what a doctor might find in my body or pain associated with a cure. In a doctor's office, there are tons of solutions and little to no celebration. If you are sick, they can fix you! Many churches are just like that—offering tons of solutions to fix you but little to no celebration when you are fixed.

Let's celebrate as a Church of the Bride of Jesus! Don't hold your joy back from Him. The best thing you can offer the world isn't information like a library or solutions like a doctor. The best thing you have to offer the world is your abandoned love for and celebration of your Husband, Jesus.

IT ALL BEGINS TO MAKE SENSE

Intimacy with God makes the entire Bible make sense. When you walk into the secret place with God, you can truly say, "The Lord is my shepherd, I shall not want" (Ps. 23). You can feel what that means in your soul. When He makes you lie down in green pastures, restores your soul, and fulfills your every desire, you realize He is all you need, that He is everything. You realize that the rest of Psalm 23 is a true statement and not just a religious ideal. Verses such as "The joy of the Lord is my Strength" become a real thing in your life. The fruits of the Spirit, as found in Galatians 5 (love, joy, peace, patience, kindness, goodness, gentleness, self-control, and faith), become real tools for you and not an unattainable ideal. The Bible begins to come to life as you experience all it speaks of. You were meant to experience these truths you read about. You surely will as you continue on this journey into intimacy with the Lord.

Nothing you experience in the Spirit will ever outshine the person of Jesus or the cross. Even if you could walk through a wall—what will that be worth unless it is bathed in love for Jesus? Even when Peter walked on water in the Bible, he did so to get to Jesus—because of his overwhelming love for Him. The spiritual and the supernatural are just byproducts of knowing Jesus in the secret place. They are an avenue for us to have a beautiful relationship with Him. They are for Him to love us and for us to love Him. The Bible says that signs will follow those who believe—not that signs will lead them who believe (see Mark 16:17 KJV). I am so wrapped up in love with Jesus it is impossible for me to think of anything deeper. In fact, it is hard for me to think of anything else I would want to pursue other than the person of Christ. Literally, nothing trumps being with Him. Don't let your zeal for spiritual things become your focus. If you do, your spirituality can actually become an idol. Keep your focus and your heart on Christ. He is the end-all. He is everything.

I encourage you to apply what you've learned here and work out your own ways to be intimate with God. Like every marriage, it is one that needs investment and time from you. It is my heart and deepest desire that this book become a resource for you to be inspired, to be encouraged, and to be guided in a practical way in this ever-increasing intimacy between you and God.

Enjoy it, and take it slow. Thankfully, this journey is one that will never get boring, will never stop getting better, and will never, ever end.

Special Thanks

I would like to take a moment to honor a few people in my life.

Jessica Money: Thank you for bravely following me into strange, and sometimes embarrassing, waters. This has been a wild ride. Thank you for sticking it out in the beginning when I didn't have my head on straight. For believing in our marriage even when I was confused about it. For loving God even when things didn't make sense and were out of balance. Your healing hands are a constant comfort to me. I can feel your love even now as I write this. I have no idea where I would be or what I would do without you. I imagine I would be in sin, or in a spiritual ditch, serving religion. You are my anchor. You are my safe place and the closest person to my heart. I feel warm and cozy thinking of how much you love me and our family. You are like a lighthouse guiding me through the fog of ministry frustrations. You keep me off the rocks and off the shore. I would have burned out and stopped running long ago if it weren't for you. I couldn't have asked for a better partner to run this race with. You are absolutely amazing. I love the simplicity you have with God. There is no fluff or shadow between you and Him. You aren't afraid of others, and you don't try to impress anyone with ministry. I love you with everything I am. You make me a better man, husband, father, and follower of Jesus Christ. I can see who the "Bride" is through you.

Madelyn, Ava, and Josiah Money: You are such good kids. I am so excited to see the Godly people you'll become. You have shown me how to worship and how to love simply. You have no agenda; you simply love me, and I love you. Stay off the paved road, and don't worry about popular opinion. Don't do ministry to impress people. Don't let fear stop you by being afraid of what people might think. Be wild and led by the Spirit of God. Honor authority, always, with everything you do. Stay away from dissentious people at all cost. In fact, run from them. Hang around those in love with Jesus, not just the "super spiritual." Blaze a trail, and stay within a community. If it ever gets tough, just know that I am always here in the cloud of witnesses cheering you on. Love Jesus, no matter what it looks like, and be brave in the face of the defeated one. Hate religion and love people. Destroy the works of the devil. Most importantly, LOVE JESUS WITH EVERYTHING IN YOU. I am always proud of you. Always remember our routine every night. I love you.

Tim and Carolyn Money: Thank you for raising me to love God. You've shown me who He really is. Everything He has is mine, and He loves me for who I am—just as you do. I know that God is big: "He is tall as them trees." I also know that He loves without condition. Something I could have never bought, read, or learned came from you—I know who He is.

Suzanne Carter: Su-man-u! Thank you for hanging in there when I was trapped in legalism and religion. I can still remember making you put on your flashers if you were speeding. I love you and enjoy all the goofy times we have together. Thank you for your grace. Thank you for loving your crazy brother. I love you. Live ferociously. No fear.

Louis and Karla Johnson: Thank you for helping me answer the Lord's call on my life. Thank you for prophesying over me and encouraging me to keep going. Thank you for trusting me and giving me a platform to shout "JESUS" from. Thank you for giving me an amazing church to grow in and be loved. The road ahead is a beautiful one.

The elders of the Vine Church: My brothers in Christ, thank you for running this race with me. It is your encouragement and prayers that have kept me going. I am honored to sit around the table with you and make plans to win this world for Jesus.

William Wood: The stories are literally endless. Thank you for looking crazy with me and answering the call of God on our lives...and just all the dang good memories. Thank you for always being an encouragement for me to constantly stay in intimacy with God. You are a forerunner; it's a blessing to run with you. Though we are miles apart, it is an honor to consider you my best friend.

Jessica Willis, Jarrod Stone, and Pattilynn Guilford: I appreciate your help in the editing process of this book. Without you this book would still be a project. Thank you so much.

Heidi Baker, Bill Johnson, and David Hogan: My heroes! You have impacted my life more than you may ever know. Thank you for your love and passion for Jesus. Thank you for inspiring me to pursue God and be myself in Him.

Teresa de Avilla, Brother Lawrence, and Joseph of Cupertino: Thank you for being forerunners so long ago. Your lives, even though we are centuries apart, have changed mine forever. I can't wait to meet you in glory.

The Bride: The brothers and sisters in Christ who have encouraged and influenced me are too many to mention. If you are spreading the message of intimacy with God, I say, "Thank you." It is an honor to live with you in a time such as this.

Appendix A

A GOOD FOUNDATION, PART 1: A PLACE TO BEGIN

One of the first real jobs I ever had was building houses with my uncle's dad. This was some of the hardest work I have ever done in my life. I quickly learned that my boss could work harder than me, even though he was more than twice my age. I also learned that he had a unique way with directions. A photographic memory, slight telepathic abilities, gigantic muscles, a doctorate degree in communications, and multiple sets of clothes are all helpful prerequisites for this job. I left at lunch for class one hot summer day, having sweat through three shirts. This man was still hard at it when I left. He taught me to work harder than I ever thought I could. He taught me to work in the dirt where most people would give up. Because of him, I am not afraid of work and perseverance.

In all seriousness, he played a huge part in helping me become a man, and I am thankful. One thing I would learn about house building is that anytime a house is built, the foundation must be built first, and it must be built solid. Let's cover some basic foundational material from which we can build on for furthering your relationship with Christ. First, let's think about a few basic facts that we know to be true.

First, the Father, the Son, and the Holy Spirit are all one person: "Hear, O Israel: The Lord our God, the Lord is one" (Deut. 6:4). They are known as the "Trinity." They, as one, have always existed: "In the beginning was the Word, and the Word was with God, and the Word was God" (John 1:1). There was no beginning of time for Them; They never had a starting point. As hard as that is to understand, it must be accepted by faith. I suppose the reason why eternal existence is so hard to swallow is because most things we see and experience in life have a start and an end. The Trinity, however, does not have a beginning or an end.

Secondly, the Holy Spirit is a person. "But when He, the Spirit of truth, comes, He will guide you into all the truth. He will not speak on His own; He will speak only what He hears, and He will tell you what is yet to come" (John 16:13). "He" is just as real as your neighbor down the street.

The relationship of the Trinity is much like an egg. An egg has three parts: a shell, a yellow yolk, and the white. The three parts of the egg are in unity with one another, while at the same time making up the same entity. Unified, they serve different roles. Even though the individuals of the Trinity serve different roles, no role of the Trinity is superior to the other. Neither of the three in the Trinity created the other.

Unfortunately, for those who wish to find answers in every single thing, I've found that some things about God, notably some of the things mentioned here, are to be believed like a child believes instead of fully understood in every tiny detail. However, if you have a question about something, please pray about it, read your Bible, and seek wise counsel, and you will likely find an answer.

YOUR "TASK"

It is actually a great thing that we serve a God who is bigger than most of our immediate rational thinking. There are some things, however, that would be helpful for us to know.

The first thing to know is our *task* as Christians. To figure this out, let's look for a moment again way back to Genesis. In the beginning of what we know as time, the Father, the Son, and the Holy Spirit (the Trinity) said in unison, "Let Us make mankind in Our image" (Gen. 1:26). The human They created in that moment was created in the exact image of God. The human was created with a spirit, a soul, and a body (a three-part being): a replica of the Trinity. This three-part being was to take dominion, to rule and to reign over the earth. "God blessed them and said to them, 'Be fruitful and increase in number; fill the earth and subdue it. Rule over the fish in the sea and the birds in the sky and over every living creature that moves on the ground'" (Gen. 1:28).

The purpose of a man and woman joining together within marriage was so that they can reproduce the image of God, a child, by creating a family. The purpose of the family was to see that the image of God spread throughout the earth. Realize that when God blessed the first family and gave them the Genesis 1:28 command, He was doing so before the first sin was committed. The separation from God that would take place because of sin hadn't happened yet. The command and blessing of Genesis 1:28 was intentionally given with the intent that all the men and women on Earth would be in relationship with God in the way they were in the Garden of Eden. The command was given to men and women, who by default (naturally), would be in relationship with Him. In Genesis 1:28, God is speaking to a couple, Adam and Eve, who are in a relationship with Him and who would birth humans also in relationships with Him. Those relational beings were to fill the earth and subdue it, reproducing others in the image of God who by default would be in relationship with Him as well.

Please realize that the original assignment from God hasn't changed. It is still Genesis 1:28. However, there is one catch—sin separated man from a relationship with God. Because of sin and being separated from God, there exists a sort of "spiritual amnesia" (I do not know what else to call it). So often we spend our lives trying to discover "Who am I?" and "What am I here for?" Part of our task in reproducing the image of God is helping people overcome this spiritual amnesia. The process is referred to as "renewing of your mind" (Rom. 12:2). It's helping them realize what is already theirs through Christ. It's helping them realize that He has given them the fullness of the Godhead (Col. 2:9–10) and His entire kingdom to live inside them (Luke 17:20–21 KJV). It's helping them realize that they have been given the Holy Spirit without measure (John 3:34). It's helping them realize they have everything—all things within them—because of Christ's cross and resurrection…fullness, lacking nothing.

In the 2006 movie *Superman Returns*, there is a special moment between Lois and the flying hero. Superman takes her high above the city.

The only things visible on the ground are what is lit by streetlights and building signs. The wind howls. "Listen," says Superman in a whisper. "What do you hear?"

"Nothing," says Lois without hesitation.

After a long pause, looking out over the dark city, Superman responds, "I hear everything. You wrote that the world doesn't need a savior, but every day I hear people crying for one."

You, holding this book, are a superhero. You are part of God's plan to redeem the world. By sharing what intimacy with God has done for you, you will help others awaken to the same freedoms you will find. People all over the earth live in bondage with problems that should not affect them because they haven't heard the reality of what Christ has done for us. Ultimately, as Christians, our task is to help people everywhere awaken to knowing confidently that they are the image of God created for an intimate relationship with Him—lacking nothing because of Christ Jesus. "For we are God's masterpiece. He has created us anew in Christ Jesus, so we can do the good things He planned for us long ago" (Eph. 2:10 NLT).

Lastly, it would be helpful to know that our task and the Holy Spirit's actions are united. He wants to help us fulfill the plans of God on our life. Literally, God will help us do what He's prepared and called us to do! Consider the verse: "For I know the plans I have for you," says the Lord. "They are plans for good and not for disaster, to give you a future and a hope" (Jer. 29:11 NLT). Notice that in this verse His plan is to *give* us this future and hope.

In the following scripture, He is referred to as the "Helper." Check out the verse:

> But the Comforter (Counselor, Helper, Intercessor, Advocate, Strengthener, Standby), the Holy Spirit, Whom the Father will send in My name [in My place, to represent Me and act on My behalf], He will teach you all things. And He will cause you to recall (will remind you of, bring to your remembrance) everything I have told you. (John 14:26 AMP)

Think about it for a moment. God has plans to help us. He wants to help us achieve all He has called us to. Are you willing to receive His help? Are you willing to take a leap when you see His plan? His plan will work whether it seems logical or not. He will help you. Go for it.

NO WORRIES

As we continue building our foundation in the next chapter, some of the questions you have may be answered. Don't worry if there is doubt in your mind about certain things that are in the scriptures. As you become more and more intimate with Christ and experience His power and presence in your life, doubt will become scarce—even if you don't get every question you have answered. Don't beat yourself up for being a thinker. God loves your mind and created you to use it! Recently, I sat with a girl on the side of the pool where she was baptized. She had doubts about the power of God, His love for her, even His existence—thoughts just like you and I have had before. I encouraged her, and I will encourage you in this. We live in a place where our faith only grows with each passing day. The more you experience with Jesus, the more you will believe. For me, at first it was very difficult to not doubt that God was a healer. However, I can't doubt His power to heal and set people free anymore because I've seen it and experienced it so many times...unexplainable miracles that could only happen outside a doctor's office. I have an ever-increasing love for and belief in Christ, not only because I feel Him in my heart, but because I can see Him at work tangibly all around me on a daily basis. I believe the same will happen in every area of your spiritual journey.

A GOOD FOUNDATION, PART 2: THE LORD'S LEADING

Recall the dream for a brief moment. What I realized in my journey out of the kitchen and into the bedroom is that the will of God is not that I do everything that needs to be done for God, but that I do everything that the Holy Spirit leads me to do. Let's talk about the Lord's leading.

HALLOWEEN

On Halloween night in my sophomore year of college, we had the privilege to baptize around four or five different international students—a few of whom I had helped lead to the Lord. While praying with one of them, she looked stunned after inviting Christ into her life. All she could say was, "Everything is so colorful." God had no doubt lifted her from a dark place that had dulled her life. The baptism that night was incredible. As we left the service, I heard the Lord say, "Go to the fountain"—a central place on campus—"and worship Me." People invited me to eat with them, but I decided to go with what I'd heard God say. I invited some of my friends to go with me to the fountain, but none of them came. It was a bummer, but I went anyway.

At the fountain, I pulled out my guitar and began to worship. About twenty minutes into worship, three international students came up and began to enjoy the music. They asked, "What are you singing about? It's beautiful."

I stopped and told them, "I am singing about Jesus."

They asked, "Who?"

I said, "Jesus Christ!" I realized in that moment that they had never heard of Him before. I spent the next fifteen minutes telling them who Jesus was, then asked them, "Do you want to know Him like I do?"

They each said, "Yes!"

Right there on Halloween night at the fountain, three Chinese students, in broken English, invited Jesus into their lives. After praying with them, I was on cloud nine. I knew that the Spirit of God had drawn us there! It felt great to do the will of God. John 4:34 says, "'My food,' said Jesus, 'is to do the will of Him who sent Me and to finish His work.'"

As the international students walked off, I looked up and saw a guy running across the open area of grass about fifty yards from me toward the dining hall. I said, "Hey man!" He stopped, and I ran up to him and said, "I know this may sound weird, but can I pray for you about anything? I believe God can heal you right now."

He mentioned pain in his knees. We prayed, and God healed him. Turns out he was on the football team and appreciated the healing. I asked him where he was with God. He said he had been running from God for some time. Right there I prayed with Him, and he rededicated his life to the Lord. He said, "To be honest, you're the first real Christian I've seen in a long time."

We are to live like Jesus: only doing what we see the Father doing, being led to every action by the Holy Spirit of God. As Jesus explained, "I tell you the truth, the Son can do nothing by Himself. He does only what He sees the Father doing. Whatever the Father does, the Son also does" (John 5:19 NLT). Jesus did not take every ministry opportunity He saw; He only took those the Father led him to perform.

This Halloween night reminds me of a time when Jesus, too, was called to a fountain or a well while His friends went to eat (see John 4). In the chapter, Jesus's disciples continue on to town for lunch while Jesus, being led by God's Spirit, goes to a nearby well. There He performs one of the most remembered miracle moments of the Bible. He could have easily followed His disciples to town for lunch and possibly performed many miracles there, but following the Father's lead, He goes to a nearby town to a well and waits there. Because of what happened at that well, a city was turned to God.

GOOD WORKS

Believe it or not, you can actually do good things and at the same time be in the *wrong* when your actions aren't *led* by God. Please consider for a moment my confusion during my early years with the Lord. I attempted to do every work I could get my hands on, whether I felt genuinely led to do it or not, and it began to ruin my life. The reality is, God doesn't call us simply to *work*; He calls us to do *good works*. "For we are God's handiwork, created in Christ Jesus to do good works, which God prepared in advance for us to do" (Eph. 2:10). These good works were prepared in advance, and they are very specific to us. To do good works, we must first hear from the good God (Luke 18:19) and do only that which He sends us to do.

The Bible says that those who are led by the Spirit of God are children of God (Rom. 8:14). We become "employees" and not "children" when we work without being led. When we are led, we live as the son, daughter, and Bride of Christ God calls us to be. Everything outside of this intimate center will lead to destruction, regardless of the intent of your heart.

THE LORD'S LEADING

I've always loved getting to pray with people for what's called the "Baptism of the Holy Spirit." I encourage you to pursue that and ask God for it, along with the gift of your "prayer language." I could insert hundreds of book references and reading material here for you on this topic. However I encourage you to simply go to the Bible. Simply read the books of John and Acts, and decide for yourself if you want it. If you want it, God will surely give it to you. I have prayed with people in the most unlikely places for this gift. I have prayed with people in my car, at a gas station, in front of the library at school, in my driveway…almost everywhere.

I remember one day I got a call from a lady at work who I'd been discussing this subject with. She was at the hospital with her mom and was worried her mom would die. While we were on the phone, God said, "Go pray with her for the Baptism of the Holy Spirit right now." I had only one issue with that…it snowed that day. In Alabama, we aren't prepared to drive on ice. It made me nervous to think of driving an hour through snow. It was also in that moment that I heard another voice—the voice of a demon. The voice said, "If you go, I will kill you." I thought about these words, as would anybody in my shoes. I decided that I would leave my wife a letter before I left, just in case I did actually die somehow. She never discovered this letter, and I came home safely. That demon wanted to intimidate me into not going. My intimacy with God was producing a love and a passion for people that said, "I will go where the Lord leads, even in the face of danger." Being *led* in the center of His will is always the safest place to be, even when it doesn't seem like where He leads is possible or safe.

AM I LED BY THE SPIRIT?
While seemingly very difficult at times, being led by the Holy Spirit is very simple. We tend to dwell forever on questions such as, "Does God want me to get a new job?" or "Does God want me to join a particular ministry?" How would you feel if I told you that you can know what God is saying for each moment of your life? The reality is, if you stay in an intimate place with God, you will have little trouble deciphering what He wants you to do in situations that arise.

Consider Christ's words: "My sheep listen to My voice; and I know them, and they follow Me" (John 10:27). Sheep spend so much time with their shepherd, they know his voice. In fact, sheep will not respond to any other person's voice than their own shepherd. To follow the Holy Spirit's leading, you must know His voice. The only way you will get to know what His voice sounds and feels like is to live with Him on a personal level—a relationship filled with intimacy on a daily basis.

THE LETTER KILLS

2 Corinthians 3:6 says, "He has made us competent as ministers of a new covenant—not of the letter but of the Spirit; for the letter kills, but the Spirit gives life." In many ways early on, I ended up following biblical principles of healing and evangelism instead of the Spirit of God. Attempting to follow the teachings and scriptures of the Bible without having intimacy with God will not only kill and destroy you, but it will destroy those around you as well. I allowed the principle "to do work" be my life focus, when I should have allowed my "intimacy with God and His Spirit" to remain my priority. Had I allowed intimacy to be my priority, ministry would have happened out of the overflow from that personal place—the bedroom.

Intimacy with a biblical principle and not with the Person of Christ led me to walk in condemnation when I wasn't doing something that I thought was working for God. I would often condemn myself for staying home with my wife. I would think, *I'm supposed to be going into all the world to preach the gospel! What am I doing here? There are people out there who need me!*—never realizing that the one I was sitting next to on the couch with her arms around me needed me more than them all. She needed a good husband, and I was not a good one. There were many moments when the voice of God was saying, "Spend time with your wife tonight," but without intimacy, I could not tell it was Him.

ARE YOUR PRIORITIES IN CHECK?

I want to briefly share some thoughts on what I believe are your priorities as a Christian. When any of these three priorities are out of order, you can be sure that you are lacking in intimacy with God.

The first priority in your life as a Christian is your relationship with God—*not your work in ministry.* It's not your youth group, church, campus ministry, singing in the choir, etc., but simply your intimate personal relationship with Him.

The second priority for your life and your *first ministry* as a Christian is your family—beginning with your spouse, then your children, then your father and mother, and next your brothers and sisters. As a constant reminder that my wife and family are my first ministry, I have intentionally moved my wedding ring to my second finger on my left hand. I get questions all the time about it. I love how this simple act has opened countless doors for me to share what the secret place has done for me.

The third priority for every Christian is your ministry calling. Whatever unique work God has called you to do belongs here—in *third* place. Street evangelism, pastoral ministry, missionary work…all types of ministry belong here.

You will notice when the first priority (intimacy with God) is taken care of, the other priorities will keep themselves aligned correctly. You will also notice that fulfillment of the first priority positions you to find fulfillment in the second priority. Likewise, fulfillment in the second positions you for fulfillment in the third. When one priority begins to shift into an incorrect position, the Holy Spirit will let you know—and you will "hear" His voice, perhaps audibly, or in your heart as a feeling, or however He chooses. You will be able to tell when something displeases Him as a result of your intimacy with Him.

I had no idea that some of the things I did during this time in my life greatly displeased Him, even though I had done many great things in His name. I was a Christian living Matthew 7:22–23: "Many will say to Me on that day, 'Lord, Lord, did we not prophesy in Your name and in Your name drive out demons and in Your name perform many miracles?' Then I will tell them plainly, 'I never knew you. Away from Me, you evildoers!'"

Believe it or not, you can raise all the dead, heal all the sick, and cleanse every leper in the world, and still miss the point—God wants to know you intimately. No doubt my life would have ended this way had my wife not been there to help me wake up. While works—signs, wonders, and miracles—are a huge portion of ministry today, I can't allow these things to replace my intimate relationship with God. If I do, I have replaced the gift for the Giver. In this way, you make the gift an idol—and an idol cannot fulfill the human heart. Many of us grow weary, become burned out, and leave ministries for this very reason.

The truth is, you will never find fulfillment solely in random work as a Christian. Fulfillment begins with intimacy with God. Ministry and intimacy with God are, in fact, two separate things—although intimacy with God does lead you to do ministry and love people. Your unique calling in ministry is fulfilling *only* when it is an overflow from the place of intimacy with God.

Looking back, I realize now that I'd replaced my first priority with my third priority. My marriage was rocky for a long time because of this ministry "idol." Jess no doubt prayed every day for me to come home, to spend time with her, to do the dishes, to fold some clothes, to look at her like I did when we were dating, and for fire to come back to our marriage. I was ready to do the "great commission!" However, before I did that, God wanted me to be intimate with Him and go on a date with my wife.

THE "OTHER JESUS"

When work is raised above an intimate relationship with God, a religion is created. Religion is a different gospel (2 Cor. 11:4). It's the thought of working your way to a relationship with God through your efforts and good deeds. It is the gospel of the "other Jesus," like the one Paul refers to in the scriptures (2 Cor. 11:4). This "other Jesus" screams, "Work! Work! Work!" He screams, "Performance! Performance! Performance!" Whereas the Jesus of Christianity says, "I want an intimate relationship with you simply because I love you" (see 1 John 3:1).

Living in the religion I created, I had to perform for the approval of God—or so I believed deep down. If I wasn't interceding or healing the sick, I felt as if I were wasting my time. Every time my wife and I went out on a date, we had to pray for someone, whether I felt led to or not. Everything I did had to have a point to save the lost or heal somebody. Don't misunderstand me: while it is important to pray for people, my wife in these moments needed my full attention, not just a piece of it. The "idol" I'd set up in ministry was costing me my life and my marriage. It wasn't until the Lord separated the two gospels of "good works" and an "intimate relationship with God" that I was finally free to not only be intimate with Him as a Bride, versus an employee, but also to be intimate with my wonderful wife, Jess.

EMPLOYEE VERSUS WIFE

I knew I had more knowledge of the Bible than most people and had seen far more miracles in a short period of my life than most see in their lifetimes. But if you were to ask me if I had an intimate relationship with the Lord—out of my ignorance of what that means—I would have said, "Yes!" without hesitation. Your asking me if I had an intimate relationship with Jesus was more like you asking me if I loved signs, wonders, and miracles. What I had yet to realize was that I barely knew Him. I equated a relationship with Christ to His wealth, His gifts, and His works.

I would never have said it at the time, but in my heart, I believed I was God's *employee*. The reality is that even though all Christians are the Bride of Jesus, if they do not believe it in their hearts, they will not live like it. Your Christian walk is, in fact, a reflection of your inner belief system. Instead of living in freedom as the glorious Bride of Christ, our erroneous belief system forces us to live in the bondages of an employee. Christ said that every tree bears fruit: "Likewise, every good tree bears good fruit, but a bad tree bears bad fruit" (Matt. 7:17). In that same way, your beliefs (representing trees) show themselves in the results (representing fruit) of your life. If you believe that you're the "Bride of Christ," your life will bring the good fruit and results of the Bride. If you believe you're the "employee of Christ," your life will bring the bad fruit and results of the employee, regardless of the numbers and statistics within your ministry.

Consider the fruit your belief system has created in your own life. Do you feel you are more like an employee or Bride? As an employee, are you living with anxiety that you are not doing enough for the "boss"? Or living as the Bride, are you dwelling in the love that you can never be fired? As an employee, are you hoping to please your boss so you can get promoted? Or as a Bride, are you doing what's in your heart for your Husband, Jesus, because you love Him? Moving from the kitchen to the bedroom means that you do ministry as the Bride out of an overflow of intimacy you share with Him. Abiding in intimacy with God will ensure that you stay focused on Him and not get trapped in religion.

FASTING

While we are on the subject of works and being led, let me take a moment and bring a balance to "fasting." I struggled with this topic for some time—I suppose because I couldn't completely understand it, or perhaps it was due to the fact that some people I looked up to preached against it. I still don't completely understand it, but in its simplest definition, it involves partnering with God here on the earth through prayer. I want to encourage you to remember that the Bible is greater than anyone's opinion on the subject. Remember Christ's words:

> When you fast, do not look somber as the hypocrites do, for they disfigure their faces to show others they are fasting. Truly I tell you, they have received their reward in full. But when you fast, put oil on your head and wash your face, so that it will not be obvious to others that you are fasting, but only to your Father, who is unseen; and your Father, who sees what is done in secret, will reward you. (Matt. 6:16–18)

Please remember the only "work" you *should* do is that which the Holy Spirit leads you to do—and this includes fasting. Being led by the Holy Spirit in your fasting is the way to go. I used to fast constantly. Every forty days, I would fast some type of food or activity. My thought was that somehow if I denied myself in this way that God would love me more or empower me more. Living by this thinking made me miserable. On the other hand, I have experienced incredible things while fasting when led by the Spirit. In a led fast, the supernatural is pulled to the forefront. In fact, Christ says that some demons only come out by prayer and fasting (see Mark 9:29 KJV). Some of the stories I've shared of God's power to heal and encounters with angels actually happened during a led fast. The bottom line is, fasting doesn't work like a formula. Just because you fast for forty days doesn't mean anything spiritually unless the Lord led you to do it.

Let's look at a time when Christ fasted: the well story in John 4. Let's observe what happened, as well as His comments to His disciples in this story as they ask Him to eat. (For your convenience, I've included the chapter in Appendix D.)

In this passage, Christ Himself says that His food is to do the will of Him who sent Him. During fasting and prayer, I know that I can feel the will of God being pulled to the forefront in my life in a greater way. It is as though I can focus on His passionate-led call in a greater capacity.

Remember another story of Christ fasting in the Bible—the story in the book of Mark. Before Christ began His ministry, He went into the wilderness to fast and pray.

> Then Jesus was led by the Spirit into the wilderness to be tempted there by the devil. For forty days and forty nights He fasted and became very hungry. During that time the devil came and said to Him, "If you are the Son of God, tell these stones to become loaves of bread." But Jesus told him, "No! The Scriptures say, 'People do not live by bread alone, but by every word that comes from the mouth of God.'" (Matt. 4:1–4 NLT)

During a fast, I personally make it a point to try to fill my physical hunger with spiritual satisfaction in my relationship with Christ. Many times through intimacy with God, I have literally fasted and prayed all day and remained hunger-free.

There are also many health benefits to consider when fasting. Toxins and harmful chemicals leave your body on many food fasts. This gives your body time to clean itself, like a detox. It is beautiful to know that even in fasting God has a plan and a purpose. Don't get on the "no fasting" train as I did briefly in the past. God has a purpose for it in your life. The spiritual and physical benefits of fasting could be a book by itself.

ISAIAH 58

An entire chapter in the Bible is devoted solely to fasting. For your convenience, I have added it to Appendix E. Please check out Isaiah 58 before moving on.

In the chapter, God says that He is not interested in a fast that is full of self-harm but one that is full of faith-filled works.

> "No, this is the kind of fasting I want: Free those who are wrongly imprisoned; lighten the burden of those who work for you. Let the oppressed go free, and remove the chains that bind people. Share your food with the hungry, and give shelter to the homeless. Give clothes to those who need them, and do not hide from relatives who need your help." (Isa. 58:6–7 NLT)

In the verses that follow, God promises salvation, healing, guidance, protection, quick answers, and many other amazing things.

In regard to everything you do, including fasting, remember what Christ has to say about it in the Bible and follow the lead of His voice.

Appendix C

A GOOD FOUNDATION, PART 3: REVERENCE AND HUMILITY

I want to briefly discuss *genuine* humility, reverence, and love. It is so important to get a grasp on these three things before we come to a close. Growing up, I thought that I knew what each of these things were, and so I very rarely questioned their definitions. It wasn't until I got a little older and a little braver that I began to question three of the Church's most sacred cows.

What excites me the most about a Christian isn't the title; it isn't the Bible memorization, the zeal, or even miracles. Those things are great, but I am most excited about a person's abandonment in his or her love with Jesus Christ. I get more excited about their intimacy with God than their work for Him.

As discussed previously, humans' ultimate and fulfilling purpose is to love God intimately—everything else flows from that. This ultimate purpose can be found in the ultimate command from Jesus:

"Teacher, which is the most important commandment in the Law of Moses?" Jesus replied, "'You must love the Lord your God with all your heart, all your soul, and all your mind.' This is the first and greatest commandment. A second is equally important: 'Love your neighbor as yourself.' The entire law and all the demands of the prophets are based on these two commandments." (Matt. 22:36–40 NLT)

Intimacy with God produces a love for God that in turn produces a desire to love people and do ministry. "Dear friends, let us love one another, for love comes from God. Everyone who loves has been born of God and knows God" (1 John 4:7). Feeding the poor, Bible memorization, zeal, miracles, etc., will flow from the love that you and God share. It is common to believe that in order to share your love with God you must do ministry. However, the reality is that you must do ministry from the overflow of intimacy in loving God. "For in him we live and move and have our being" (Acts 17:28). Placing ministry ahead of intimacy can lead to religion.

CHRIST VERSUS THE TEMPLE

Consider the verse: "But I say unto you, That in this place is one greater than the temple" (Matt. 12:6 KJV). The temple in all its glory and tradition is no comparison to the person of Christ. Two thousand years ago, Judaism did not recognize Him simply because they had no intimate relationship with Him. They had a religious system of rules, regulations, robes and sacrifices—the temple. This system in their minds left little need for genuine relationship with God Himself. Not recognizing Him when He came to rescue them, they crucified Him.

We can see a pattern throughout the ages where, in a sense, God's people choose the temple and rules over an awareness of His precious presence. Unfortunately, this same crucifixion happens every week in some churches—not a crucifixion of the man Jesus, but a crucifixion of His intimate, passionate, unique presence. His presence once again is sacrificed for the sake of the temple and religious traditions. Paul warns us to be careful not to be deceived by tradition: "See to it that no one takes you captive through hollow and deceptive philosophy, which depends on human tradition and the elemental spiritual forces of this world rather than on Christ" (Col. 2:6).

BEING HUMBLE AND REVERENT

Religious traditions often go under the radar as attempts in showing "humility" or "reverence" toward God. Humility and reverence are not found in a broken facade, a broken demeanor, or a crushed spirit. They are not marked by a suit, a tie, or khakis. They can't be found in self-mutilation, self-hatred, self-denial, or other religious attempts. They can't be found in an old wooden pew, a golden cathedral, or the largest mega church in the world. They can only be found in abandoned, intimate love with God.

True humility and true reverence involves leaving every reservation and every held-back place in abandoned adoration and enjoyment of King Jesus. Any counterfeit cannot contain the glory of God and is nothing more than a religious attempt to please God or to please other people.

"WE DON'T DO THAT HERE!"

I recently spoke with a young person from a local church who told me of a time when she was worshiping God with her hands raised. She said an angry deacon quickly crept around the room to where she was and pulled both of her hands down. She was scolded: "We don't do that here!" She quickly collected her things and ran out of the sanctuary, crying. The experience angered her, turning her off to the church's entire denomination. It wasn't until later when she came to a small group at our church that she finally felt accepted—she had nearly given up on God because of a religious tradition.

Unfortunately, the deacon involved with this experience sacrificed the presence and worship of God for a tradition of man—a symptom of religion. I hope the deacon at the church she attended learns to embrace the uniqueness of a person's adoration of Jesus. We were all created differently, so we will each have a unique way we like to worship, pray, and interact with Jesus.

LOVING PEOPLE FOR WHO THEY ARE

Truly being intimate with God stretches us beyond our comfort zone. God gently asks us to embrace things that are new to us with an open heart and to accept people for who they are. Try not to put down someone's prayer, worship, or uniqueness with Christ just because it is different from what you're traditionally used to. If we're not careful, we can make the same mistake the Jews made when they crucified their God. You unknow-ingly and metaphorically can sacrifice Christ for your own preferences and traditions by saying "that's not of God"—when, in reality, God could be all over it.

Everything must be proven right and good by God's word—not a pref-erence, an assumption, or a tradition. In the same way that God turned Judaism upside down with the early Church, He is now turning "religious" parts of Christianity upside down with those who are truly intimate with Himself. "But when they did not find them, they dragged Jason and some brethren to the rulers of the city, crying out, 'These who have turned the world upside down have come here too. Jason has harbored them, and these are all acting contrary to the decrees of Caesar, saying there is an-other king—Jesus'" (Acts 17:6–7 NKJV). By turning them upside down, He is bringing correction and balance where it is needed within the body of Christ. This is especially true as it pertains to unbiblical preferences and traditions that are oftentimes held as doctrine or foundational belief.

BE UNIQUE, BUT BE HONORABLE
If you are in a church where you traditionally worship in a certain way, but you feel led to worship or pray in another, then go for it in an honorable and biblical way. All authority is delegated by God. "Let everyone be subject to the governing authorities, for there is no authority except that which God has established. The authorities that exist have been estab-lished by God" (Rom. 13:1). Be sure to honor the authorities God placed in the church you attend while at the same time realizing that He created you to be you. You should love the Lord with all your heart, all your soul, all your mind, and with all your strength (see Luke 10:27), whatever that looks like to your unique relationship with God. Embrace your uniqueness, and you will experience the presence and power of the Lord's intimacy in your own life.

As we bring "A Good Foundation" to a close, please hear my heart: do not dishonor those God has placed in authority in the church you at-tend. If you are uncertain about expressing your love for God in a certain way, please approach an authority of the church you are a member of and ask if that is OK there. Also, if you are in a church that doesn't adore God in the way you want, *don't* automatically assume God wants you to leave that church. God may want you there anyway. Seek Him and His decision before deciding to find another church. Offense at a brother or a tradition is not a reason to leave a church. The voice and leading of God is the only reason to leave or join a body of believers.

Thank you for reading this three-part foundational material. My prayer for you is that you grow as you are mentored and serve in your local church. Please do not consider this *all* you need to know as a believer. However, please know that I consider it an honor to help you get started.

As your next step I encourage you to get baptized and get involved in a church, a community you can call home. Refer to this book often as you like and always remember to stay in the secret place with God.

JOHN 4:1-42

[1] Now Jesus learned that the Pharisees had heard that He was gaining and baptizing more disciples than John—[2] although in fact it was not Jesus who baptized, but His disciples. [3] So He left Judea and went back once more to Galilee.

[4] Now He had to go through Samaria. [5] So He came to a town in Samaria called Sychar, near the plot of ground Jacob had given to his son Joseph. [6] Jacob's well was there, and Jesus, tired as He was from the journey, sat down by the well. It was about noon.

[7] When a Samaritan woman came to draw water, Jesus said to her, "Will you give Me a drink?" [8] (His disciples had gone into the town to buy food.)

[9] The Samaritan woman said to Him, "You are a Jew and I am a Samaritan woman. How can You ask me for a drink?" (For Jews do not associate with Samaritans.)

[10] Jesus answered her, "If you knew the gift of God and Who it is that asks you for a drink, you would have asked Him and He would have given you living water."

[11] "Sir," the woman said, "You have nothing to draw with and the well is deep. Where can You get this living water? [12] Are You greater than our father Jacob, who gave us the well and drank from it himself, as did also his sons and his livestock?"

¹³ Jesus answered, "Everyone who drinks this water will be thirsty again, ¹⁴ but whoever drinks the water I give them will never thirst. Indeed, the water I give them will become in them a spring of water welling up to eternal life."

¹⁵ The woman said to Him, "Sir, give me this water so that I won't get thirsty and have to keep coming here to draw water."

¹⁶ He told her, "Go, call your husband and come back."

¹⁷ "I have no husband," she replied.

Jesus said to her, "You are right when you say you have no husband. ¹⁸ The fact is, you have had five husbands, and the man you now have is not your husband. What you have just said is quite true."

¹⁹ "Sir," the woman said, "I can see that You are a prophet. ²⁰ Our ancestors worshiped on this mountain, but you Jews claim that the place where we must worship is in Jerusalem."

²¹ "Woman," Jesus replied, "believe Me, a time is coming when you will worship the Father neither on this mountain nor in Jerusalem. ²² You Samaritans worship what you do not know; we worship what we do know, for salvation is from the Jews. ²³ Yet a time is coming and has now come when the true worshipers will worship the Father in the Spirit and in truth, for they are the kind of worshipers the Father seeks. ²⁴ God is spirit, and His worshipers must worship in the Spirit and in truth."

²⁵ The woman said, "I know that Messiah" (called Christ) "is coming. When He comes, He will explain everything to us."

²⁶ Then Jesus declared, "I, the one speaking to you—I am He."

²⁷ Just then His disciples returned and were surprised to find Him talking with a woman. But no one asked, "What do You want?" or "Why are You talking with her?"

²⁸ Then, leaving her water jar, the woman went back to the town and said to the people, ²⁹ "Come, see a man who told me everything I ever did. Could this be the Messiah?" ³⁰ They came out of the town and made their way toward Him.

³¹ Meanwhile His disciples urged Him, "Rabbi, eat something."

[32] But He said to them, "I have food to eat that you know nothing about."

[33] Then His disciples said to each other, "Could someone have brought Him food?"

[34] "My food," said Jesus, "is to do the will of Him who sent Me and to finish His work. [35] Don't you have a saying, 'It's still four months until harvest'? I tell you, open your eyes and look at the fields! They are ripe for harvest. [36] Even now the one who reaps draws a wage and harvests a crop for eternal life, so that the sower and the reaper may be glad together. [37] Thus the saying 'One sows and another reaps' is true. [38] I sent you to reap what you have not worked for. Others have done the hard work, and you have reaped the benefits of their labor."

[39] Many of the Samaritans from that town believed in Him because of the woman's testimony, "He told me everything I ever did." [40] So when the Samaritans came to Him, they urged Him to stay with them, and He stayed two days. [41] And because of His words many more became believers.

[42] They said to the woman, "We no longer believe just because of what You said; now we have heard for ourselves, and we know that this man really is the Savior of the world."

Appendix E

58 "Shout with the voice of a trumpet blast.
Shout aloud! Don't be timid.
Tell My people Israel of their sins!
[2] Yet they act so pious!
They come to the Temple every day
and seem delighted to learn all about Me.
They act like a righteous nation
that would never abandon the laws of its God.
They ask Me to take action on their behalf,
pretending they want to be near Me.
[3] 'We have fasted before You!' they say.
'Why aren't You impressed?
We have been very hard on ourselves,
and You don't even notice it!'
"I will tell you why!" I respond.
"It's because you are fasting to please yourselves.
Even while you fast,
you keep oppressing your workers.
[4] What good is fasting
when you keep on fighting and quarreling?
This kind of fasting

will never get you anywhere with Me.
[5] You humble yourselves
by going through the motions of penance,
bowing your heads
like reeds bending in the wind.
You dress in burlap
and cover yourselves with ashes.
Is this what you call fasting?
Do you really think this will please the Lord?
[6] "No, this is the kind of fasting I want:
Free those who are wrongly imprisoned;
lighten the burden of those who work for you.
Let the oppressed go free,
and remove the chains that bind people.
[7] Share your food with the hungry,
and give shelter to the homeless.
Give clothes to those who need them,
and do not hide from relatives who need your help.
[8] "Then your salvation will come like the dawn,
and your wounds will quickly heal.
Your godliness will lead you forward,
and the glory of the Lord will protect you from behind.
[9] Then when you call, the Lord will answer.
'Yes, I am here,' He will quickly reply.
"Remove the heavy yoke of oppression.
Stop pointing your finger and spreading vicious rumors!
[10] Feed the hungry,
and help those in trouble.
Then your light will shine out from the darkness,
and the darkness around you will be as bright as noon.
[11] The Lord will guide you continually,
giving you water when you are dry
and restoring your strength.

You will be like a well-watered garden,
like an ever-flowing spring.
¹² Some of you will rebuild the deserted ruins of your cities.
Then you will be known as a rebuilder of walls
and a restorer of homes.
¹³ "Keep the Sabbath day holy.
Don't pursue your own interests on that day,
but enjoy the Sabbath
and speak of it with delight as the Lord's holy day.
Honor the Sabbath in everything you do on that day,
and don't follow your own desires or talk idly.
¹⁴ Then the Lord will be your delight.
I will give you great honor
and satisfy you with the inheritance I promised to your ancestor
Jacob.
I, the Lord, have spoken!"

Appendix F

PSALM 91 (NJB)

[1] You who live in the secret place of Elyon, spend your nights in the shelter of Shaddai,

[2] saying to Yahweh, 'My refuge, my fortress, my God in Whom I trust!'

[3] He rescues you from the snare of the fowler set on destruction;

[4] He covers you with His pinions, you find shelter under His wings. His constancy is shield and protection.

[5] You need not fear the terrors of night, the arrow that flies in the daytime,

[6] the plague that stalks in the darkness, the scourge that wreaks havoc at high noon.

[7] Though a thousand fall at your side, ten thousand at your right hand, you yourself will remain unscathed.

[8] You have only to keep your eyes open to see how the wicked are repaid,

[9] you who say, 'Yahweh my refuge!' and make Elyon your fortress.

[10] No disaster can overtake you, no plague come near your tent;

[11] He has given His angels orders about you to guard you wherever you go.

[12] They will carry you in their arms in case you trip over a stone.

[13] You will walk upon wild beast and adder, you will trample young lions and snakes.

[14] 'Since he clings to Me I rescue him, I raise him high, since he acknowledges My name.

[15] He calls to me and I answer him: in distress I am at his side, I rescue him and bring him honour.

[16] I shall satisfy him with long life, and grant him to see My salvation.'

HEBREWS 11

11 Now faith is confidence in what we hope for and assurance about what we do not see. [2] This is what the ancients were commended for.

[3] By faith we understand that the universe was formed at God's command, so that what is seen was not made out of what was visible.

[4] By faith Abel brought God a better offering than Cain did. By faith he was commended as righteous, when God spoke well of his offerings. And by faith Abel still speaks, even though he is dead.

[5] By faith Enoch was taken from this life, so that he did not experience death: "He could not be found, because God had taken him away." For before he was taken, he was commended as one who pleased God. [6] And without faith it is impossible to please God, because anyone who comes to Him must believe that He exists and that He rewards those who earnestly seek Him.

[7] By faith Noah, when warned about things not yet seen, in holy fear built an ark to save his family. By his faith he condemned the world and became heir of the righteousness that is in keeping with faith.

[8] By faith Abraham, when called to go to a place he would later receive as his inheritance, obeyed and went, even though he did not know where he was going. [9] By faith he made his home in the promised land like a stranger in a foreign country; he lived in tents, as did Isaac and Jacob, who were heirs with him of the same promise. [10] For he was looking forward to the city with foundations, whose architect and builder is God. [11]

And by faith even Sarah, who was past childbearing age, was enabled to bear children because she considered Him faithful Who had made the promise. ¹² And so from this one man, and he as good as dead, came descendants as numerous as the stars in the sky and as countless as the sand on the seashore.

¹³ All these people were still living by faith when they died. They did not receive the things promised; they only saw them and welcomed them from a distance, admitting that they were foreigners and strangers on earth. ¹⁴ People who say such things show that they are looking for a country of their own. ¹⁵ If they had been thinking of the country they had left, they would have had opportunity to return. ¹⁶ Instead, they were longing for a better country—a heavenly one. Therefore God is not ashamed to be called their God, for He has prepared a city for them.

¹⁷ By faith Abraham, when God tested him, offered Isaac as a sacrifice. He who had embraced the promises was about to sacrifice his one and only son, ¹⁸ even though God had said to him, "It is through Isaac that your offspring will be reckoned." ¹⁹ Abraham reasoned that God could even raise the dead, and so in a manner of speaking he did receive Isaac back from death.

²⁰ By faith Isaac blessed Jacob and Esau in regard to their future.

²¹ By faith Jacob, when he was dying, blessed each of Joseph's sons, and worshiped as he leaned on the top of his staff.

²² By faith Joseph, when his end was near, spoke about the exodus of the Israelites from Egypt and gave instructions concerning the burial of his bones.

²³ By faith Moses' parents hid him for three months after he was born, because they saw he was no ordinary child, and they were not afraid of the king's edict.

²⁴ By faith Moses, when he had grown up, refused to be known as the son of Pharaoh's daughter. ²⁵ He chose to be mistreated along with the people of God rather than to enjoy the fleeting pleasures of sin. ²⁶ He regarded disgrace for the sake of Christ as of greater value than the treasures of Egypt, because he was looking ahead to his reward. ²⁷ By faith

he left Egypt, not fearing the king's anger; he persevered because he saw Him who is invisible. [28] By faith he kept the Passover and the application of blood, so that the destroyer of the firstborn would not touch the firstborn of Israel.

[29] By faith the people passed through the Red Sea as on dry land; but when the Egyptians tried to do so, they were drowned.

[30] By faith the walls of Jericho fell, after the army had marched around them for seven days.

[31] By faith the prostitute Rahab, because she welcomed the spies, was not killed with those who were disobedient.

[32] And what more shall I say? I do not have time to tell about Gideon, Barak, Samson and Jephthah, about David and Samuel and the prophets, [33] who through faith conquered kingdoms, administered justice, and gained what was promised; who shut the mouths of lions, [34] quenched the fury of the flames, and escaped the edge of the sword; whose weakness was turned to strength; and who became powerful in battle and routed foreign armies. [35] Women received back their dead, raised to life again. There were others who were tortured, refusing to be released so that they might gain an even better resurrection. [36] Some faced jeers and flogging, and even chains and imprisonment. [37] They were put to death by stoning; they were sawed in two; they were killed by the sword. They went about in sheepskins and goatskins, destitute, persecuted and mistreated—[38] the world was not worthy of them. They wandered in deserts and mountains, living in caves and in holes in the ground.

[39] These were all commended for their faith, yet none of them received what had been promised, [40] since God had planned something better for us so that only together with us would they be made perfect.

I would love to hear your story! Please feel free to contact me:
Visit my website: woodymoney.com
On Facebook, Instagram, Twitter, and Snapchat: @woodymoney